CW01081361

Kakwenza Rukirabashaija

THE SAVAGE AVENGER

theworldiswatching

© 2023 Kakwenza Rukirabashaija (www.kakwenza.de)

First Published as The Savage Avenger in 2023

Cover Illustration: Chris Ogon Atukwasize
Portrait Photo of Kakwenza: Lookman Kampala

Published by theworldiswatching
Produced by BoD - Books on Demand, Norderstedt

ISBN (print version): 978-3-9825132-2-5
ISBN (e-book): 978-3-9825132-3-2

All rights reserved. No part of this publication may be reprinted or reproduced in any form or by any means, without permission in writing from the publisher and author.

This is a narration of the harrowing torture which I was subjected to when I was arrested on 28th December 2021 on orders of Gen. Muhoozi Kainerugaba, the commander land forces and also son to despot Yoweri Kaguta Museveni, president of the Republic of Uganda.

We took our legitimate frustrations to the streets,

and they called us violent.

we were shot at with impunity.

teargassed and murdered. Imprisoned.

A law was introduced,

called public order management Act,

to criminalize freedom of assembly.

We took our nonviolent opinions to social media.

They branded us extremists

Yet we are only extremely angry.

Then they called it hate speech.

Hating oppressors is not hate speech.

It is blowing off steam.

You want to murder, torture, force us into exile

and when we protest

You say it is hate speech?

Poem by Kakwenza, 2023

For my children; the Kakwenzas

Tolerance will reach such a level that intelligent people shall be banned from thinking so as not to offend the imbeciles.

Dostoyevsky

We live in a time where intelligent people are being silenced so that stupid people won't be offended.

Unknown

FOREWORD
BY PROF. HELEN EPSTEIN

In Uganda, night dancers are ordinary people who become possessed by evil spirits. In the wee hours, they wake up, throw off their clothes and run around naked. Sometimes they eat corpses and cast spells on living people. I first heard about night dancers decades ago when I was working at Uganda's main referral hospital and teaching at a university there. Most of the Ugandans I knew joked about night dancers, the way we in the west tease children about ghosts. But some people seemed to believe they really existed.

I'd forgotten about night dancers until I read the work of the award winning novelist, lawyer, human rights activist, torture survivor and PEN honoree Kakwenza Rukirabashaija. He's written three books: a novel satirizing the rise of Ugandan dictator Gen. Yoweri Kaguta Museveni, now in his 37th year in power; a memoir about being tortured for writing that novel, and *The Savage Avenger*, an account of being tortured again for tweets referring to Museveni's son General Muhoozi Kainerugaba as an *"obese inebriated curmudgeon"*. Together these books provide a valuable introduction to Uganda's current politics - if what goes on under such a ruthless regime can be considered that.

The Greedy Barbarian, published in 2020, recounts the life story of Kayibanda, son of a commercial sex worker and grandson of a night dancer, who grows up to become the cruel war-mongering ruler of a fictional African country. His story bears many resemblances to Museveni's. Like Kayibanda, Museveni is rumored to have been born outside Uganda and raised by an impoverished pastoralist stepfather. Like Kayibanda's, Museveni's education was sponsored by a prominent Ugandan elder, whom he later betrayed; like Kayibanda, Museveni is rumored to have had a multifaceted sex life, such that the identity of his son Muhoozi's mother is subject to speculation; like Kayibanda, Museveni is believed to imagine himself an heir to the Chwezi, an ancient clan of tall and lanky mystical warrior kings who ruled over much of modern day Uganda, Rwanda, Burundi, northern Tanzania, eastern Congo and South Sudan and were said to be so fearsome they wore fringe over their eyes because if you looked right into them you'd shrivel up and die. Like Kayibanda, Museveni worked briefly for Uganda's intelligence services, was later appointed defense minister, ran for Parliament, lost mightily, seized power anyway through an insurgency, declared he would not inflict violence on his own people and then proved to be even crueler than his predecessors. Like Kayibanda's, Museveni's security forces have rigged elections, tortured and killed members of the political opposition, instigated civil war and launched brutal rebellions in neighboring countries where the Chwezi are said to have once held sway. Like Kayibanda, Museveni has presided over colossal corruption, wrecked a promising economy and trapped his nation in debt. Like Kayibanda, Museveni has enjoyed the support of the World Bank and international donor nations, including the United States, United Kingdom and European Union members, whose diplomats smile and fistbump with him before the cameras as though they themselves had been bewitched by the Ugandan head of state.

In order to appreciate Rukirabashaija's wit, it's essential to understand the extreme politeness of Ugandan culture. You feel it at once, as soon as you step off the plane or cross the border. Practically everyone is charming, humble and kind and tries to be helpful. Even Museveni's goons are polite, except when in the process of torturing someone or shooting into a peaceful crowd with impunity.

Good manners are part indigenous custom, part legacy of colonialism. Once the dirty work of conquest was accomplished, the British who ruled Uganda from the 1890s to 1962 relaxed the color bar far more than in their other African possessions. Missionaries sipped sherry with elite Ugandans in their private quarters, and the governor invited them on hunting trips and entertained them at tea and cocktail parties.

In this genteel atmosphere, rudeness became a political weapon for pro-independence Ugandans. In response to a dinner invitation from an Anglican Bishop, one rebellious Ugandan responded with eighteen pages of vitriol, accusing the Bishop of helping the British steal Uganda's land and minerals.

This is the tradition to which *Greedy Barbarian* belongs. Rukirabashaija and a growing number of other Ugandan writers and artists, including the redoubtable academic Stella Nyanzi, who, in one of her poems likened Museveni to *"a pair of buttocks"* - use rudeness not just as political entertainment, but as a courageous form of dissent.

Greedy Barbarian was an instant hit in Uganda, until the regime banned it and pulped every copy in the bookstores. For Museveni, the book was unpardonable lese majeste, and Rukirabashaija soon found himself in the custody of Uganda's Chieftaincy of Military Intelligence (CMI). For over a week, he was detained in a "safe house" - one of an unknown number of secret, ungazetted torture chambers around the country. There, he was forced to lick the filthy floor of an interrogation room, had his head stuck in a full toilet and was beaten so badly that his eyes and kidneys were damaged. He was then injected with unknown substances, waterboarded, forced to kneel on gravel until his knees bled and fed beans containing weevils.

Rukirabashaija's plight attracted attention outside of Uganda, and he was eventually released. *Banana Republic: Where Writing is Treasonous*, a non-fiction account of his torture ordeal appeared in 2020, upon which he was arrested and beaten once again.

Then, in December of 2021, came the *"obese inebriated curmudgeon"* tweet concerning Museveni's son Muhoozi. At the time tensions with neighboring Rwanda were high, and Muhoozi, who envisions himself as Uganda's future leader, had been tasked with trying to de-escalate the situation by negotiating with Rwanda's leader Paul Kagame. Rukirabashaija is tall and thin and looks a bit Rwandan. He had also traveled to Rwanda from time to time. Muhoozi seems to have concluded that he was a Rwandan spy, on a mission to undermine the Uganda-Rwanda detente. Hence another round of torture ensued.

This time, Rukirabashaija was abducted by Uganda's Special Forces Command (or SFC) - an elite military unit that operates outside of Ugandan law under the control of Museveni's family. SFC officers have received training from high level US military commanders and carry sophisticated Israeli weapons, including Uzis, Tavors and Galil-Ace rifles. But their treatment of Rukirabashaija was weirdly low tech. Armed with pliers, operatives plucked chunks of skin from the author's back, thighs, arms and other body parts. Then they took him to meet Muhoozi, who patiently explained the benefits of using his literary gifts to praise the regime, instead of criticizing it.

None of this surprised me. Countless Ugandans have been subject to even worse abuses at the hands of Uganda's security forces. But what took me aback is that Muhoozi's goons also forced Rukirabashaija to dance all night with a jerrycan of water on his head. As I read this, those night dancer stories from decades ago came back to me. The symbols and rituals of this part of Africa are truly mysterious. Was Muhoozi trying to turn Rukirabashaija into an evil night dancer like himself? Or did Muhoozi believe Rukirabashaija already was a night dancer, putting curses on the ruling family? Whatever Muhoozi and his goons were up to, it was not successful. Their prisoner managed to flee and now lives in Europe with his wife and children.

What Uganda's rulers don't get is that clobbering words is impossible. As long as there is a pen left on earth, anger, sorrow, laughter and cries will slip under every doorway, and between the bars of every prison. They will escape every hammer, and cross every border, even if the authors are no longer around. In this way, they are truly supernatural.

 *Prof. Helen Epstein is a visiting professor of human rights and global public health at Bard College. She is the author of Another Fine Mess, a book that brilliantly exposes the bloody results of America's exclusive diplomatic relationship with Uganda's President Yoweri Museveni.*

UNSHAKABLE

What is freedom to write without a right to describe things in their veridicality and sincerity? Without a right to describe someone's unfeigned physical appearance? Without describing someone's bona fide behavior? Without describing the dictatorship, oppression, greed, cataclysm, pogrom, inhuman treatment, unlivable conditions imposed onto us by our leaders? Without such freedom, savage leaders and their chamchas grow unclipped feathers and society sinks into the abyss of imbroglio. Freedom to write is the beginning of real freedom, and denying writers this freedom is the beginning of anarchy.

Leaders with absolute power that cannot use it to improve the lives of their countrymen but instead use it to loot, plunder and practice savagery, hate the idea of writers diagnosing their disingenuousness, as far as honoring the social contract between them and the electorate is concerned. Social protest literature has a way it diagnoses, professionally, the imbecility of savage despots to the understanding of everyone. It is the wind that blows off the robe of hypocrisy for people to see hidden streaks of misanthropy that shapes their power. No despot has ever won a war against writers. King Leopold's plunder of Congo and murder of 10 million Congolese was exposed by writers like Willian

Henry Shepherd, George Washington Williams, E.D Morel and several others. All these writers never capitulated to threats and the mighty power of their pen was triumphant.

The troubles between the Ugandan state and I began when I published my debut novel, *The Greedy Barbarian*. It was meant to shine a beam of light into the hellholes of impunity for readers to see what we are encapsulated in as a country. Before that, the state had not minded about me. I was not a threat and my humble home had never been besieged by the military. It was a month after publishing it that my home turned into a barracks. When I came out of prison, I narrated the dreadful torture I endured inside the Chieftaincy of Military Intelligence (CMI) dungeons, in another book, *Banana Republic – Where Writing is Treasonous*. Then I was picked up again and tortured and charged bogusly with *"inciting violence and promoting sectarianism"*.

I did not give up even when the state bought off all my books from the shelves and threatened to pull them down from Amazon where I was selling them to the outside world.

The president must have been deceived by his un-intelligent intelligence team that to silence me, they would send me a pulchritudinous damsel to do the job. After a while, I received a phone call from a lady who identified herself as Jojo. She asked to meet me for lunch and asked that I carry my debut novel. I asked whether she had read Banana Republic - my torture memoir - and she answered in affirmative. So that meant that she came to know about the former after reading the latter. The day came and we met - in the alfresco side of Café Javas, Kamwokya. I autographed for her the book and she pulled out a wad of crispy yellow notes from her purse and handed me UGX300,000, and also paid for the whole bill of what we consumed. When I asked why she had to pay all that for a novel of UGX50,000, she retorted that she is rich and that she was buying me Namaqua Wine as her kind and eleemosynary consolation for all the horror I went through. Jojo told me that she was 33-years (my age-mate then), though she looked younger. She had that youthful and exuberant sparkle of about 24-years. Her radiant, glistening and spotless thighs and beauty were a sore sight for my ogling eyes.

I hadn't saved her number yet, but I saved it proudly that evening. She would call often to check on me, caring like we had known each other for long, or like we were dating. But I played elusive and lackadaisical, wondering what her intentions were.

After a month without meeting again, Jojo asked me out to lunch. But I told her that I was in the countryside and busy at the Court lumbering with state-inspired persecution. She asked me when I would be in Kampala and I reluctantly promised her that I would call as soon as I got into the city.

Jojo and I would often engage in coquetry chats and, as a matter of confession, she was beginning to move me. I began longing to talk to her. I blame myself for leading her on and giving her audience to entangle me. When I met Jojo on a Tuesday for lunch, she asked me what I did for a living and how much I earned. I told her and she laughed at me with a lot of spite on her face. *"How do you survive on such a picayune salary, Kakwenza?"* She asked with concern. I was reticent because I felt like she was mocking my pecuniary misfortune that was temporary. I was even ashamed of the British tailored suits I would wear all the time. Her laughter reeked schadenfreude.

She asked if she could get me a good job and of course I answered in affirmative. I flinched like a surprised toad when she mentioned that I would be earning ten times more than I was earning. That night I didn't sleep. I thought that my life was going to switch from destitution to riches in just a fortnight. The whole time, I was thinking about paying off my debts in a few months of working and buying land for farming high value crops. We shared a lot from lunch time up to 8pm. When I excused myself to leave, she offered to drive me home in her ML Benz, but I turned down the offer saying that I had a car – which kind of discombobulated her. She wore an exasperated face as she bid me goodbye. I drove home and she also drove the opposite direction.

After two weeks, I began to realize that Jojo was setting me up for something cruel. Thanks to Ruhanga and my ancestors for they blessed me with a sixth sense premonition of imminent disaster. The job she had gotten for me, I would earn ten times indeed, plus enjoying other privileges attached to it, with a proviso that she would get for me a fully furnished house, of which she would have exclusive possession of the keys and I would not be allowed to have visitors. And that she would check in anytime of the night.

It came to my attention that her phone number wasn't even registered (I checked using mobile money) and upon googling her name or even searching on Facebook, the process was fruitless. The number wasn't even on WhatsApp.

Jojo had told me that her other name was Nakachwa, but she looked and spoke English like a Munyarwanda.

The last time we met, I attempted to be a detective by stealthily taking a picture of her. I picked my phone from the pocket, feigned a phone call and while carrying the device to the ear, clicked the camera and perfunctorily took a picture of her. Like a commando in the detective Hollywood movies, Jojo Nakachwa grabbed my phone. Then she deleted the photo, her number and cleared the entire call log. The speed with which she did all that is indescribable. It caused a bit of a scene and people around stared at us in shock. She grabbed her bag and walked out. I have never seen or heard from her again. She was probably a highly trained mercenary hired to finish me off without trace.

In early December 2020, I went on a holiday to Rukungiri, my ancestral home in Western Uganda, after spending a month on a sickbay in the time following my eye surgery. I received a call while I strolled about on the hill admiring nature and the sunset behind the beautiful hills of Kigezi. The voice on the other end was of a woman who had called to tell me that I was needed at State House

Nakasero to meet with a big man. I had just been, a month before, announced by the English PEN as the winner of the PEN Pinter Prize for International Writer of Courage.

"I am out of Kampala and broke," I said.

"We can arrange transport for you," she responded.

"I have my own car and driver," I rebutted.

"I mean, if you do not have fuel, we can send it to you via Mobile Money," she said.

Her voice was euphonious, not because it carried the president's message or financial relief but she spoke like those ladies who market insurance premiums and Bank loans. Even if you do not need the money or insurance cover, her magnetic voice will charm you into signing for that rubbish.

After about five minutes, I indeed received five million shillings on my phone, with 'fuel' as the reason. That was a lot of money because my car consumed only three hundred thousand Ugandan shillings for five hundred kilometers. I drove to Rukungiri town the following morning and withdrew the money to zero balance. I switched off the phone and drove to Rwanda - just a few kilometers away from Rukungiri - and spent a week thinking about idiots who thought that they would bait me with picayune millions. I chewed the money to the last shillings which I used to buy fuel back to Kampala.

When I returned to Kampala and switched on my phone, the lady called me immediately and asked what had happened. I had no answer except to listen to her euphonious voice. When the reticence on my side became unbearable for her, I could really hear her breathe with disappointment for a failed co-optation. She was really disappointed but for her sweet voice, I apologized. If it had been a man, I would have told him to go to hell. I am capable of burning bridges with a male chamcha but not with a female, you know!

A week later, I received another call from a woman who duped me that she was buying my books for a school or schools and asked me how many I had in total and I perfunctorily told her 1,000 copies. When she asked if I would want cash on delivery or bank transfer, I chose the latter and indeed she transferred the fifty million shillings into my bank account. The books were delivered to the address which she provided the following day. My delivery guy later told me that where he delivered the books, there were several Toyota Hiace vans (drones) and UPDF trucks, somewhere in Bugolobi - a Kampala suburb. The money was blocked by the Financial Intelligence Authority and the bank required a letter from the depositor, pursuant to The Anti-Money Laundering Act, 2013. I was asked to prove the source and purpose of funds that are more than $10,000.

When I reached out to the mysterious woman depositor, she told me, with indescribable braggadocio, that I either cooperate with her as an agent of the regime or forget about the money.

"What is expected of me?" I asked, foolishly.

"Begin writing in favor of his excellency the president," she retorted.

I regretted why, when she asked whether I would want cash or bank deposit, I chose bank deposit. I had heard stories of people being hacked and cash robbed, so I thought that I was circumventing such a possible disaster. I had even made calls to my creditors assuring them of debt clearance.

It was a very difficult decision for me to refuse such a huge amount of money despite the conditions. I refused to kowtow to her inveigle. It was an intricate decision to be obdurate. It was like a starving dog refusing a fatty piece of steak.

THE ARREST

The worst came to the worst when I took it to my Twitter page, calling out the kleptocratic gerontocracy of Yoweri Kaguta Museveni with scathing fulmination. I described the president as a despot, murderer, plunderer and election thief who is glooming his obese curmudgeon and inebriated incompetent son Muhoozi Kainerugaba to inherit him as though the presidency is a hereditament. That was the last straw. Immediately, the Special Forces Command (SFC), the branch of the army tasked with providing security to the president and his immediate family members, plotted my arrest.

According to the statement which was submitted to court by the prosecution team, Maj. Denis Kakande was instructed by Gen. Muhoozi Kainerugaba to execute the mission to arrest me. The former is a personal assistant to the latter.

On 28th December 2021, I bade goodbye to my wife and children and dogs after spending a few Christmas days with them. Immediately after breakfast, I pulled out the phone to call our family driver to come and drive me to the taxi park in Iganga, but my wife insisted that she would drive me herself though she was unhappy that I was leaving home after spending a few days with them. Her unhappiness was legitimate, but I needed to rush and finish up some office work in Kampala.

The decision to leave was actually impromptu because I had promised my children that I would be with them through the new year, for my wife and I often celebrate our wedding anniversary on 31st of December. Even the phone calls I was making with friends and relatives depicted that I was still relaxed in the village. Little did I know that my calls were being tapped.

I alighted from a taxi at Lugogo and crossed the road to the side of the mall and waited for the Taxi Bolt which I had ordered. I had never seen a taxi driver who looked like a well-connected and high-ranking army official with a mustache, but since it was Bolt, I took it with equanimity and did not say a word until he dropped me at my home on Arches Close, Kisaasi. Oftentimes when you get a driver from the Uber or Bolt apps, they want to negotiate the price by increasing what is shown on the app, but this one did not. As I was entering my house, the gateman too was opening for the mysterious driver to go. I was careworn by the journey and decided to take a siesta first and then see what to do next in the evening.

At about 3pm, I was woken up by an awful din outside and the clamor of too many shoes on the ground. The bedroom door was open, and the main exit and entrance door closed from inside. I tiptoed out of the bedroom and looked through the living room window. I was shocked to see a barracks of soldiers outside, led by the same Bolt driver. He was pointing at the door saying, *"I have dropped him here and saw him enter this house."* He still wore the same clothes and sunglasses.

I counted twelve UPDF (Uganda People's Defense Forces) men in uniform, and eight other officers in civilian clothes. They were all armed with machine guns and some had pistols clutched on their trousers' waist belts. Then there was one holding a sledgehammer.

Dumbfounded, I didn't know what to do next. It was too late for me to escape because my house had one door which was both entry and exit. The hatch to the scuttle attic in the bathroom was at an unreachable height and I needed at least something to step on to reach there. The kitchen cabinets were very small considering my height. I wouldn't fit in there. There was nowhere to hide. I was girdled in my own house.

Kakwenza Rukirabashaija ✔
28. Dezember 2021 · 🌐

I'm under house arrest. Men with guns are breaking my door. They say they're policemen but are not in uniform. I've locked myself inside.

😮😢😡 1.519   498 Kommentare   111 Mal geteilt

I grabbed the phone and called my friend Ronald Muhinda, who told me that he was a bit far and that it would take time to arrive at my place since he had no car but said that he would immediately inform the world about the siege. I went ahead and fumbled with the phone and called my boss who also told me that she was driving with the kids for the weekend and made a U-turn back. Then at last I called my lawyer Eron Kiiza who asked me to remain on the phone with him until he arrived. After posting on Facebook and Twitter about the siege, I deleted all the social media apps. I hid my computer in the closet and another phone in the breast pocket of one of the suits. That is when a soldier who was peeping in the bedroom through the open bedroom window actually saw me and alerted others who were on the other side of the front.

"Can you please open the door now? You are under arrest," one officer commanded while banging the door. He sounded drunk.

I refused to open and instead added a lock on the door. Their commander, a potbellied officer in civilian clothes, warned that he would break my legs upon entering the house when I asked for their Identification and arrest warrant. By this time, they had already broken two windowpanes to have a glimpse of the inside of my house and it was through this opening that they were threatening me.

Section 4 (3) of Police Act Cap 303 provides that no person shall arrest, detain, or institute Criminal Proceedings except as is provided for under a written law or the Constitution. These were savages sent to brutalize me by their leader, the most high savage Muhoozi Kainerugaba.

Upon knowing that I was determined not to let them in and the fact that I was on phone with my lawyer, they had to act quickly. The first attempt to break the door failed, so they hit the window and broke the glass and all the shads poured into the house. Then next were the burglar proofs, and then the whole window fell into the house. The two young men in civilian clothes jumped in and punched me in the stomach and used their gun butts to hit my back and ribs. My phone was confiscated while I talked to my lawyer.

I fell down helplessly and caterwauled tunelessly with pain.

"Where is the key?" one brute asked.

"It is in the pocket," I capitulated.

I was later handcuffed and pulled out of the house and commanded to sit on the lawn. In an apartment detached from my house, upstairs on the third floor was a lady recording everything. When she was seen, she was forced to delete her gallery. Her house was invaded immediately, and she was forced to apologize after a few slaps and threats. I wondered if what they were doing was right, why did they not want to be filmed?

"Have you checked the house properly?" The potbellied man asked another one who was closing the door.

"Yes sir," he affirmed.

I doubt he did. If he had, he would not have missed my other gadgets.

In the next minutes, I was bundled into a waiting white drone (Toyota Hiace Van), which had parked at my gate in the company of another of the same make and two other small white and gray Toyota Corolla cars.

Having been arrested several times before, I knew what was next. When I was blindfolded with a thick black beanie and strings pulled and knotted around my neck, it did not surprise me. I was used to it. They didn't tell me why I had been arrested nor did they show me any arrest warrant. All this happened in full view of my gateman and other neighbors.

The drone roared into life, reversed and sped off uphill, following other vehicles which were leading the way. After about 10 minutes, I heard the gate open and the drone pulled over into the parking lot. I was pulled out of it and pushed into another which started and sped off. I couldn't see anything, but the area was as quiet as a cemetery in the middle of the night. It was away from the busy road, and I later came to learn that it is the Crime Intelligence Directorate in Naguru, headed by Col. Chris Serunjoji Ddamulira.

In about fifteen minutes we were on the road again, and I could hear the taxi touts haranguing passengers to board to Kawempe, then later to Mityana-

Mubende. My decent sense of geography confirmed that we were driving on the Northern bypass and connecting to the Entebbe Express highway.

INSIDE THE TORTURE DUNGEONS

After about an hour from the time I was arrested, we reached a place which I presume was a busy Military barracks because there was a lot of Kiswahili brouhaha – a language commonly used by soldiers in Uganda. As I was being pulled by the collar through the lawn, following the person pulling me sheepishly without seeing anything, I could hear, in the distant interior, a chopper landing. For a moment, in that state of agony, I thought that I was being taken to the chopper to be flown somewhere. The pulling on the lawn was replaced by a paved way and now my bums were sliding on the hard surface while another person hit my feet hard. I was sweating.

"Remove your shoes," he ordered. By that time, I had only one, another had slipped out during the pulling. As I stepped out of it, he checked my pockets and removed a leather wallet which had several Bank and ID cards and two crispy notes of 50,000. He asked me to remove my wedding ring and hand it to him, which I did resignedly. "I have your spectacles, ring, wallet and sandals, sindio?" he asked. *"Yes,"* I said inaudibly.

I was pushed into a room like a sack of potatoes. The South African reggae music was blaring in the room as my captors began to hit my ankles severely with either a baton or bludgeon. The beating lasted for about seven to ten minutes. I was later abandoned there, on the floor, groaning in excruciating pain. The music was very loud, and I doubt they could listen to me.

Since my face was covered too, they missed seeing the heavy flow of tears from my eyes. In about an hour, my legs and knees were all swollen as though I had elephantiasis. I would touch them and feel the spongy protuberance and the pain was excruciating. Without giving any reason, they beat me while I was handcuffed and blindfolded as the music blared on maximum volume so that they could not hear my wailing. I sprawled and wailed and by the time they stopped the beating, my body was all on fire and weak. I could not stand up when I was instructed to. I simply fell asleep. The beater would shout instructions in my ear, and the stench from his mouth was malodorous.

After an hour or so, he instructed me to sit facing the corner and brought some food for me. He adjusted the beanie so that I could have access to the mouth. Somehow, I managed to see the cold posho and beans mixed together in a mound looking like food thrown in a garbage bin. I also saw his gray boots and the camouflage uniform tucked right into them.

"Wewe simama," he shouted into my ear.

I struggled to get up. When I had staggered and acquired standing balance, he instructed me to dance to the blaring music.

"Afande, you can see that my legs are swollen from the beatings, I cannot manage," I said.

I don't know if he heard what I said, but he simply began to beat me again while shouting and I began dancing painfully.

The last time I had danced was many years before at our primary leavers' party, and I had vowed never to dance again. I think I was 14 years, but taller than everyone, including teachers. Upon stepping into the dance hall, I attempted some Michael Jackson breakdance moves which I had watched in videos like *Dirty Diana, Thriller, Smooth Criminal*, among others. Accidentally, my hand swatted into a boy's head with a whack, the leg stretched into his crotch with an indescribable whoosh, and he groaned. I was shown exit, and I vowed never to dance again. Now here I was, handcuffed and blindfolded and being forced to dance again to reggae music in prison with swollen legs.

That regrettable evening, I danced the whole night. I sweated and my mouth dried like wood despite drinking water almost every five minutes from the jerrycan placed near me. I pleaded for mercy because my legs were swollen, but the soldier told me that if I were tired of dancing, I would get down on plank position and do push-ups. I accepted at first hoping that he would let me do thirty of them and rest, but I collapsed at the fiftieth and he beat me up to continue until I pleaded to resume dancing.

In the middle of the night, I was given only an hour to sleep. Before I could catch sleep, as I was nursing the pain, he came and asked me to get up and dance again. The tiles were very cold, no mattress or blanket. Just tiles. I came to realize that maybe the purpose of keeping me dancing was to keep me warm because a minute or two into rest, I would begin shivering from coldness. At first, I thought that I was alone, but later I realized there were others. When I was getting down to put my bruised ribs on the tiles, I adjusted the beanie and counted about six others who were also blindfolded and handcuffed and had also been told to rest. Oftentimes our heads would knock while looking for the jerrycan of water.

While I was going through all that torture, I wondered what kind of laws applied to Uganda and whether such people really knew that the Constitution of the 1995 Republic of Uganda as amended, the entire chapter four of it protects everyone from inhuman treatment. The Prevention and Prohibition of Torture Act, 2012 and other statutes pari materia, prohibit such savage treatment of human beings. But it seems President Yoweri Museveni and his son Muhoozi Kainerugaba are sadists that derive pleasure from seeing the suffering of critics.

The main purpose of these laws is to check such barbarism and whoever is displeased by another individual's behavior is supposed to use the law, not the stone age and archaic methods of torture or mob justice.

Article 24 of the Constitution of the Republic of Uganda 1995 as amended, guarantees freedom from torture, cruel, inhuman or degrading treatment or punishment. This guarantee is absolute and in fact prohibitory as per Article 44 (a). Consequently, under Article 24, Parliament enacted the Prevention and Prohibition of Torture Act 2012, under which Section 2 (1) defines torture as any act or omission by which severe pain or suffering, whether physical or mental, is intentionally inflicted on a person by or at the instigation of or with the consent or acquiescence of any person whether a public official or other person acting in an official or private capacity. Further, Section 3 provides for prohibition of torture and the enjoyment of the right to freedom from torture shall be non-derogable.

I would sometimes be forced to carry a twenty-liter jerry can full of water on my head and dance with it through the whole night. They would force me to do push-ups or planks whenever I would tell them I was tired. I would sweat, the sweat would stop, my mouth would dry and still continue to dance vigorously at gunpoint.

The first two days in the dungeon, all I was thinking about was to get freedom and then flee the country. Initially, I had vowed never to abandon the struggle and go to exile even after the past two arrests and grievous torture but this time, I could not wait to get out and run for my life. I was there reconnoitering in the thoughts where to pass, through the Democratic Republic of Congo Eastern porous borders or Rwanda since I am lanky like Rwandese and also speak their language fluently. The whole plan was in my head and now I was hatching how to execute it while still encapsulated in this hell of a dungeon.

One morning I had just sat down from the night's dancing, to eat porridge and bread which had been served to me and a soldier pulled me by collar and dragged me through the doorsteps, then another set of steps and through the carpeted ground, and into something like an interrogation room. He pulled me without minding my head knocking edges of walls and doors. It seems the entire building is carpeted with wool and it smelled nice, different from the room which had noisy music 24/7. This one was quiet, and a smell of fried eggs and milk wafted into my nostrils while I was being dragged like garbage.

"Kneel down," he instructed me, while at the same time forcing me to do exactly what he had told me. My knees were swollen and painful. I felt like the bones were falling apart upon kneeling straight as

I had been instructed, but any slight hesitation would call for severe beating.

"Mr. Kakwenza Rukirabashaija, today you are going to tell me why you hate Muhoozi Kainerugaba and his father, the president. The fountain of honor," a vibrant voice spoke over yonder.

Before I could respond, I was slapped five times in the ears and the world around me was spinning. I could feel my brain melting with the avoirdupois of the masculine slap. As I was stammering and composing myself to answer, he asked me what had happened to my feet. He reached closer and began poking them with something which had a touch of a baton and said that he would break them if I did not give them satisfactory answers.

"If you have problems with the army commander and his father, the president, I want you to tell me right now," he commanded and walked away. I heard him slump into a chair and whisper in a conversation. There were a few of them, but it seems it was only one person doing the talking and others stood by my side to rain slaps and beatings on me. I could sense it. I could also sense that there was a powerful figure in the room. I was blindfolded, yes, but there must have been someone big present ready to listen to me.

For the start, the interrogation was centered on my book – Banana Republic where writing is treasonous – which narrates the harrowing torture I went through at CMI (Chieftaincy of Military Intelligence) Mbuya in April and September 2020. They contended that the publication caused them sanctions from the Western governments, and that they are ashamed of it.

"I want you to remove the book from Amazon right now and you stop selling it," he ordered, and the ones beside me did the beating.

"But sir, I was beaten before for this book but now you are beating me again," I pleaded.

"But you have continued to sell it, even on Amazon it is there selling and you are posting about it," he rudely interrupted. *"How do you explain that?"*

"I do not know, sir," I said. It is as though I had poked my hand into the anus of a leopard. The beatings I received for that statement alone, I could feel my body organs dislocating especially the heart, lungs and stomach. I could feel them inside my body.

When he switched the interrogation now to the unflattering tweets I had posted, describing the president's son, I knew that I was dead. I had to explain every bombastic English word in the tweets. They had printed out all the unflattering tweets and I could hear them flipping pages of papers and shooting questions. They beat me like a snake and my buttocks were burning. I wailed like a child. I could no longer kneel; I was ready to die. Then I was allowed to sit, but the buttocks were on fire and I felt like each body part was breaking away from me. It was like my heart and brain had betrayed other body parts and were being punished for it, and eventually were breaking away – to free themselves.

The interrogator asked me who sponsors my twitter diatribes against the first family to the extent of body shaming them. I honestly had an answer to say, but it only stopped in my mouth. I didn't spew it out because if I had, I would have been killed right there. I was right in captivity of his chamchas. The empty-headed ones moreover, bereft of any humanity in them.

"How can a whole soldier and army commander be obese; does he not exercise daily? Or what he knows is to live a sedentary lifestyle of drinking alcohol, glorifying violence, living off our picayune coffers, threatening cowardly and at the end receiving promotions from his father," the invective almost escaped my mouth.

During interrogation, oftentimes the interrogator would mention names from different foreign embassies to ascertain whether I knew or were in contact with them. The only person I knew from a bunch of names which they asked me was Gilbert Cathal, the diplomat in charge of Human Rights and Democracy at the European Union mission in Uganda. Others I had never met or interacted with them. I had only met Gilbert once when I returned from prison the second time and I never met him again.

There is an article I had written in the newspapers questioning the excellency of the president and they read it to me in full and asked me if it was me who brought the idea that the president of a country must be called his excellency and now was withholding the suggestion and why.

The article goes:

"Each and every one has one or two things that discombobulate them. For me, I have come today to tell you about what bothers me – to address Gen. Yoweri Museveni as his excellency or fountain of honor.

The noun excellency comes from excellent which means the quality of being outstanding or extremely good as per Oxford English dictionary. So, the title 'excellency' is a form of address given to presidents, vice presidents or ambassadors whose characteristics are first class, superiority in virtue and not mediocre.

Such titles should be a reserve for leaders who exude exceptional character, not these pathological liars who group themselves with guns to catapult a government then agglutinate themselves into power as malignant leaders who do not value reciprocal obligations but want allegiance from a disgruntled population whose discontentment is looked upon as recalcitrance.

Our allegiance shouldn't come on a silver plate as though we are docile. In thinking that we are docile, that is why they act as though they are not bound to the reciprocal obligations which come with leadership positions.

We were told that to err is human but as Barack Obama once said, leadership comes with responsibility to admit mistakes and to speak the truth all the time. If a leader speaks the truth, behaves like a human being, admits mistakes, presides over a country where critics are not pariahs – why not address them in their excellency?

What is excellent in a leader who, after taking an oath of office, stands in a bulletproof cage to threaten the extinction of opposition or those who speak truth to power? We have seen other leaders giving inaugural speeches promising to be presidents of all countrymen and women regardless of whether they voted for them or not but for Museveni thinks that to command respect and allegiance, he must threaten his critics and in doing so, he loses the excellence and honor to be addressed as his excellency or fountain of honor.

I mean, if you promise to use your power as a president to crush me or to make me a pariah in my own country, why should I not wonder at the excellency title you own?

What is excellent in a leader who takes all the credit but transfers the blame to other people?

My issue is: we live in a country where a president is a liar, never admits mistakes, re-appoints looters (I do not know whether he loves the slogan 'a looter continua'), glorifies extrajudicial murders as long as they are opposition and demonstrating their disgust against his warped methods, violates or bends the law to favor his exaggerated self-importance – and still he is addressed as his excellency or fountain of honor? What is excellent in such actions?

Leaders who transude excellence, know when to go, they do not bribe lawmakers to remove the limits from the supreme law such that they cement themselves in power until they die. The dogma of heaping encomiums on a leader regardless of their flaws which they do not admit is for cowards. These leaders need to be told the truth in lieu of being their desperate chamchas.

If other presidents are excellent in their characters and they admit mistakes and speak the truth, respect the law, and treat citizens equally – then they qualify the titles excellency and fountain of honor but these ones here who do contrary to what is expected of a leader, personally I have no shame and fear in addressing them as despots or in accordance with their actions.

One cannot steal public funds meant for putting drugs in hospitals and due to lack of the same, patients die and you refer to such a leader as an honorable person. What is honorable about stealing?

There is a dictum in Ruhororo that 'Okubaziika heihi nikyo kyikutuma banuuka' literally means that the reason the dead smell even after the burial is because they are buried in shallow graves.

There is no shame in addressing Museveni as a despot and a failure. I do not need to be rich or high profile to remind the president that he is not excellent, his character is paradigmatic of stinking dictatorship and maladministration."

The only question I answered without them beating me was when they asked me whether I was Rwandese and when I answered in the negative, they asked me why I am lanky and why I frequent Kigali. *"I often go to Kigali just to rest,"* I answered. *"Why Kigali, not Nairobi?"* he shot back. *"Because I prefer Kigali to Nairobi,"* I answered.

All the time they were asking me these questions, there was little or no chance for me to answer and when I did, the responses were not from my heart but from a simulacrum of myself sheathed in pusillanimity of maltreatment. After all, I had nothing to answer to such wastrels whose well-being depended on being chamchas of rogues like moribund Museveni and his curmudgeon son. Their work to deflect criticism by inflicting severe pain onto critics in lieu of taking it as advice, or with equanimity seemed to be a full-time job.

I had to explain in detail the meaning of each word they did not understand in the article. By the time

I was dragged back to the cell or dancing hall, I was regretting why my mother had brought me into this world. It was a whole day of beating, and now I would spend another night dancing with a jerry can of water on my head. What a pseudo liberation these men said they brought to us in 1986!

I regretted why I was a citizen of such a country. I vowed not to look back after getting released. I was ready to renounce my citizenship. It was now a burden, a burden of nationality.

HOUSE SEARCH

I was picked up again from the dungeon, dragged by the collar, very early in the morning and I guess it was about 4 am, because the breeze was still wheezing and the smell of the lake would penetrate through the beanie and into my nostrils while being dragged in the alfresco of the barracks lawn. The frogs in the nearby swamp or water source were croaking innately. For a moment, I thought that they were taking me to Court and I somehow felt a cowrie of hope running through my chest and thoughts. There was a chopper either landing or preparing to take off. At first, I thought that it was for me to be airlifted in and then the person who was pulling me led me into the car and ordered me to sit down on the floor of the aisle and not in the seats. And when my long-swollen legs stretched to the front, they were hit with the gun-butts and for the entire journey I was coiled. Numb.

I didn't know that the brutes were taking me for a house search at my second home in Iganga Municipality, about 160 km or so from where I had been detained incommunicado. When the vehicle pulled over in front of my gate, one of the soldiers pulled and removed the beanie from my head and ordered me to move out of the drone. There were about eight soldiers armed with guns and all dressed in black with masks to hide their mean looking faces. About five others were in civilian clothes and armed with pistols, and three anti-terrorism police officers also armed to teeth. The scenario attracted the attention of all the neighborhood and they swarmed the place asking what was going on. There were two other vehicles, one of which was a Police lead car. My wife and children began to cry upon seeing me limping and looking indescribable – walking with excruciating pain and all the shame. They had last seen me healthy and well a week before, during Christmas. Now the person who had been brought home wasn't known.

"Every time you take my husband, you bring him looking terrible like this. What kind of human beings are you?" Eva shouted.

I could see the rage in her eyes, she was annoyed with the demons but she did not know what they were.

"Control your wife before we beat her up," said a soldier.

"You beat her for what? What has she done to you? Aren't her grumblings valid?" I asked.

"Continue, you will tell us when we take you back," another masked officer said.

I had no words to tell my children and wife. My wife was becoming more obstreperous and unmanageable. Barefooted, I walked through the driveway and entered the house, followed by my captors. It is then that I recognized Bill Ndyamuhaki of

Cybercrime Intelligence and he is the one who led the operation for the house search. I had met this plump brute before in CMI Mbuya barracks and also at the Special Investigations Unit in Kireka a year before and his face was still fresh in my eyes.

"We have come here to do a house search. We want all the gadgets, guns, and everything you think is relevant," Bill foolishly declared.

"My phone was taken by the guys who arrested me from my Kampala house. Here, I have nothing," I said with anger.

"I want your computer, Kakwenza," he said. *"Please hand over your computer which you use to write your books,"* he added, pleading.

"My computer was confiscated the last time I was arrested and I have not bought another one," I said.

"A whole writer, you have no computer?" he said.

I had hidden my computer in the closet in my house in Kampala and it was by sheer luck that when they arrested me, they did not see it. So now they thought it reasonable to drive all those kilometers, waste fuel to my other home to turn it upside down for gadgets and guns.

Bill Ndyamuhaki and his fellows searched the house for hours, there was nowhere that his fat short hands didn't reach. Our bedroom, children's bedrooms, visitor's bedroom, butler's bedroom, toilets, laundry room, dinning, living room, book-shelf – everywhere, including the car. He searched until I could see his elephantine bums sweating and began grumbling when he found out that the search was in vain.

The search was unwarranted contrary to the law. Under the Criminal Procedure Code Act, Laws of Uganda, no search can be carried out by the police without a Search Warrant issued by Court. These search orders are obtained under section 70 of the Magistrates Courts Act and section 7(2) of the Criminal Procedure Code Act of 1950, and are granted by the magistrates' courts.

These brutes were not even Police but presidential guards masquerading as Police. Only Bill Ndyamu-haki was known to be working with the Criminal Investigations Department (CID). They did not even allow us to call my lawyer, Eron Kiiza, to update him on the development as the law requires.

The only thing they got from the house was my wife's Samsung tablet, which she had not used since I bought it for her on our honeymoon in Dubai back in 2017.

I looked terrible. I had spent the whole time without a proper bath. I had not brushed my teeth. I looked like a caricature of my former self. The clothes were shredded and bloodied from the beatings. I looked scrawny, when the handcuffs were removed so that I could access the bathroom and also change clothes. One army officer escorted me and stood in the bathroom. I urinated blood. I craned my head to look at him askance whether he had seen what was flowing out of me and indeed he had seen to his utter shock. He did not say a word. I undressed myself, and for the trouser I had to struggle with it because the ankles were swollen and so it was very tight. I sat on the tiles and he helped me pull it. I stood under the cold shower and washed off the sweat that had accumulated for days, dried blood and all the suffering. He waited and looked on until I finished showering, shaved armpits and scrotum, pubic hair and brushed my teeth. I did all that to provoke him but he was cool. He looked at me as I got hold of the buttock to shave off the hair in the cleavage. He smiled when I held the scrotum with care and clean-shaved it. He only broke the silence when I began to smear my body with lotion.

"Men do not do that; it is a women's thing," he said foolishly.

"I am not men, I am Kakwenza," I responded.

"You are stubborn, that is why they have beaten you to that extent. They will kill you if you don't mind your words," he warned.

"You would not find loss because we are not related," I said while stepping out of the bedroom towards the laundry room.

In the corridor, I met my wife and whispered to her to take pictures of my clothes and send them to my lawyer via WhatsApp.

"I am urinating blood, do not forget to tell him."

News

He Was 'Wearing Blood' Instead Of Clothes, His Entire Body Was Full Of Deep Wounds: Tearful Kakwenza's Wife On Tortured Husband

January 5, 2022   974   3 minutes read

Kakwenza Rukirabashaija's Clothes socked in blood from alleged torture by state operatives

That's the only time I talked to my wife privately because the rest of the time, the bodyguard would pry or want to know what I was telling my wife.

Bill Ndyamuhaki was visibly disappointed that the house search did not go as expected. He thought that he would either find a gun, drugs, my computer or any other incriminating evidence to corroborate their propaganda that I was bankrolled by the president of Rwanda, Paul Kagame, to do espionage for him. But, I wondered, how could they think of such a thing? Me without any military or espionage training to be an agent of another country? Most of my 33-years in this world have been spent in school hungering for education and more education. I have not wasted any of it in becoming a chamcha of hypocritical individuals or aspiring for any political office.

When I had finished taking milk and juice and eating bananas, I was forced to sign on the document on which they had listed all the stuff they took from my house. My wife too signed. They had called the area chairman and he signed too. I was later handcuffed again, blindfolded in front of my children and wife and then led to the drone at the gate. Were they now taking me to my Kampala house? I thought to myself. I was satisfied and fresh from the shower after a long time. I sat on the floor of the car, fixed between the seats in the aisle and slept off for the whole journey.

I was awoken by an officer who hit me to get up. He removed the blindfold and asked me to get out. It was night out but luminous dark. We were now at Kibuli CID Headquarters. I was ushered into a spacious office. I ensconced myself in a two-seater palatial leather couch and Bill Ndyamuhaki brought me a bottle of water to drink. He sat opposite me in a spring office chair, leaned his head on the head rest and took a swig on the water.

"So now Kakwenza, I will need passwords to your phone, twitter and email," he said, in a threatening voice as though he meant to say that if I refused, he would take me back to the torture chamber.

His bodyguard picked a pen and paper from the table and handed it to me to scribble down the passwords. This is illegal, but do these fools follow any law? Right from arresting me up to now, everything was illegal.

I was forced to write down the password to my phone, twitter account and email address. The law protects me from having to give testimonial evidence – by duress – that would be incriminatory.

Outside, it was dark, the night was still young and I figured it was about 9 pm or thereabout. He also made statements in my name and forced me to sign against them on false belief that I was being released. When I was led outside, I thought that they would release me. When I was handcuffed, I thought I was going to be put in Police cells but instead I was blindfolded and bundled into the drone again. It took about an hour or two for the drone to snake through a traffic jam to the Special Forces Command (SFC) dungeons in Entebbe. Back to the room with blaring music, I was served with cold posho and beans and as soon as I had emptied the plate, the beats awaited me to dance.

MORE TORTURE

A day after the fruitless house search in Iganga, I was picked from the dungeon, dragged through the stairs and taken back for interrogation. I was instructed to undress and mistakenly I thought they wanted me to remove the trousers and shirt only. As I attempted to indicate to them that I was handcuffed, an impatient brute who stood behind me ripped the clothes off my body and I stood naked in their midst. The only cloth I had on me was the blindfold.

"Kakwenza, you have refused to tell us who is behind you, who your sponsors are, but this is your last day to live," a vibrant voice announced.

"I have told you nothing but the truth, there is no one who gives me anything," I said.

"Did you know during Amin's presidency there was a person called Maliyamungu? Do you have an idea what he would do to a person like you?"

At your age, where did you get the money to build all that beautiful house? Where did you get money to buy two expensive vehicles? Your house is beautiful with expensive furniture," he said.

"Did you see his library? Too many books," another one chipped in.

59

"That is where he gets all the hard English he posts on twitter," another one said, and they all laughed in concert.

"How can you be a young well-read man with such progress in life and resort to abusing the president and first son?" he asked.

"I abused no one. I only used English to describe them," I said.

"Can't you describe them nicely?" he asked.

For gods' sake how would you describe the smell of pig shit nicely without mentioning how malodorous it is? I thought and almost said it. I was tired. Tired of living. Tired of being tortured yet I couldn't summon myself out of pusillanimity.

I was asked to lie down prostrate and I did. I only remember brutes descending on me with what felt like wires and mutilating my back and buttocks. Then someone was busy plucking flesh from my thighs with what painfully felt like pliers. In about five minutes I lay in a pool of my own blood. Some were hitting my nails and ankles as hard as hammer-strikes, and shouting at me to speak or I would die. The blood was too much and I could feel it, some got into my mouth. The brutes beat me until I became numb, lifeless and unconscious. Up to now I ask myself whether the brutes who mutilated me have families and go back to them in the evening. I keep asking myself what they did with the flesh which was picked from my thighs, or what they did with all the blood which oozed out of me.

By the time I gained consciousness, I lay prostrate in the same dungeon blaring with music, where I had been picked from. I had no idea about the time. Someone, a doctor maybe, was busy treating my mutilated body. The deep and fresh dermatological ulcerations were being treated with painful liquids and powder.

I could not sit or stand. Every part of me was painful and swollen except the head. He would inject me six times every day in the legs and on the buttocks, wash the wounds at least twice a day and apply medicine. He would bring me tablets and capsules to swallow – 17 in number and at once – at least three times a day. So, in a day I would swallow 53 tablets and capsules and my body would be injected 36 times. All this was done without my consent.

The amount of tablets and capsules I was swallowing were like food. Imagine 56 of them in total every day!

The first two or three days were very difficult because I could not move. The wounds were still fresh and bleeding all the time. I would use my clothes to clean the blood from the tiles and also use them as a pillow. All the time I was on the very cold tiles shivering because of coldness as they had told me that the cold tiles were good for healing.

I would only sleep on my stomach because it was the only side that was not mutilated. Other parts had very deep wounds, including on the right arm and it was very difficult to turn sides, not even sleeping on the side.

The brutes who mutilated me were now treating me to heal. From then, they would leave me to lay down on cold tiles and that is when I got the opportunity to look at my fellow handcuffed and blindfolded victims who danced all the time. I would watch them shake their bodies endlessly in tattered clothes. They would only sit down when food and porridge was served, or when the person on duty would be merciful to allow them to sleep for an hour or two.

White Porridge would be served early morning with bread, then lunch at about 3pm and dinner at 5pm. Finishing off the food was compulsory. The sauce of beans would oftentimes be mixed with silverfish or eggplants and the posho was generally not bad as compared to the one which is fed to remanded or convicts in the gazette prisons.

I do not eat any type of fish, so one day I told the officer on duty that I would not eat the food because there was silver cyprinid fish and it smells bad for me. *"Pick posho and beans only and leave the fish alone then,"* *he* said rudely.

I would look at the small fish with silver scales and popped eyes and little open mouth and wonder if it was disemboweled before drying, or if it is eaten with its innards like grasshoppers.

Bathing was once a day, and I would not consider it as bathing really. We would line up blindfolded, hold each other's shirt or trouser and walk in line. The first person would carry the jerry can of urine. The detached bathroom and toilet were about 200 meters away from the dungeon. We would line up at the door and each person would be given three minutes to bathe. By the time one would finish undressing and using the toilet, he would be ordered to get out. And then one would dress up and blindfold themselves! After being mutilated, I stopped going with my fellow prisoners to bathe because I was just like a catatonic person unable to move.

After about two days, the person who was treating me told me that the wounds were drying and that I would soon be fine.

"No one knew that you would survive. Man, you are very strong," he confessed.

"Why did they do this to me?" I asked.

"There is a lot of pressure outside. Man, you are popular, so they think someone or a group of people are behind you," he said.

He sounded calm and I wondered why he was working for brutes. He was not rude like others, and oftentimes he would sympathize with me. He would bring me glucose water every day and advise me that it was good for my health. I would attempt to steal a glance at him in vain. I only managed to see that he wore only one pair of black shorts every day. His legs were dark and boney and his toes stunted and gray. He spoke good English with a touch of Luo accent and was cognizant of medical terms.

One evening, as I was seated facing the wall and looking at my swollen ankles and deep wounds inside my thighs through an adjusted blindfold, he brought for me a black trouser without a zip and button, and a brand-new yellow polo shirt – with a picture of Museveni embroidered on the front, and on the back of it was *VOTE MUSEVENI*. He told me to wear them.

"I am taking you to meet someone important, so you must at least cover your nakedness," he said.

The t-shirt was tight-fitting, but the trousers were very small. What mattered, he said, was to encase myself in clothing. He helped me get up, walked me out of the dungeon and took me to an office. I was still blindfolded but not handcuffed. I was asked to kneel down and I did, with difficulty.

"Kakwenza, is the doctor treating you well?" a voice asked, with a heavy Rukiga accent.

"Yes sir," I said almost inaudibly.

"Now, the big man wants to forgive you, but we must record you asking for forgiveness," he said. I wanted

to ask which big man and forgiving me for what, but I swallowed the words and kept quiet. I would not risk being hammered again. And why was he interested in forgiving me after mutilating me?

"If you accept to stop writing against the government and cooperate with us, we shall recruit you into the UPDF legal department and life will be good," he promised.

"That is if you stand by your word," he added.

"We know where your family is including your children and even if you run away, we shall find you and kill you," he threatened.

"You are dealing with a government in power which is capable of doing everything within its means to eliminate uncooperative people like you," he continued.

"Do not think that you are special to be begged or chased around," he said.

The blindfold was thick, but I could feel the effect of the video recorder in front of me and its light into my eyes.

I apologized to despot Yoweri Kaguta Museveni and his cannibal brute son Muhoozi Kainerugaba just to get out of that filthy place. It was very painful to humble myself and kneel down, raise my hands and say out apologies before my tormentors.

"I, Kakwenza Rukirabashaija from Rukungiri do hereby apologize to you, president Yoweri Kaguta Museveni and Muhoozi Kainerugaba. I promise that I will never criticize nor write about you again. Please find a place in your heart and forgive me." I LIED.

They recorded it twice and there was silence for about five minutes. Then I heard another voice.

"They have accepted your apology and they have forgiven you so you will be released."

At that particular moment, I was cornered and could do anything to circumvent more trouble. So I was a yes man now, but with a lot of rage in my heart. I kept on imagining how they tortured me while blindfolded and handcuffed, as if I were a demigod so powerful to break the chains and beat them up like Hercules of Greek mythology.

I was taken to a different room and ordered to sit down. This particular one smelled nice with a scent of expensive designer perfume hanging in the air. The floor was carpeted with wool and I ensconced down and stretched my legs to my comfort. The blindfold was removed and I saw myself ensconced in the middle of luxury furniture and beautiful walls decorated with portraits of Yoweri Kaguta Museveni and other army officers I did not take time to recognize.

As I was still darting my eyes hither and thither, they landed on a person in civilian clothes who sat across. No one would fail to recognize Lt. Muhoozi Kainerugaba. Even in the darkest night he would be recognized by at least a smell of alcohol and the braggadocio or entitlement in his utterances. He was busy on a computer conceivably reading something or pretending. With an overgrown mustache and beard, clean shaven head, obesity and big-boned shoulders encased in a gray polo-shirt striped with black, he sat there like a big warty toad. I could not believe my eyes.

"You can go now; I will call you later," he told the person who had brought me in, without shifting his eyes from the computer.

I did not turn to see the person behind me, but I heard him salute and stamp his boot down, walk out and close the door behind him.

"Tell me, Kakwenza. What is it that you want in your life? Everything that you want and we shall see," he attempted to mansplain me.

Now, I was debating in my heart whether to pour out the anger and ask him why he needed to first torture me before asking me such patronizing questions. I took it with equanimity.

"You have seen how your fellow opposition people make noise, then suddenly come to work with us, so the ball is in your hands," he added.

"Actually, every opposition person gets money from me and Mzee so you are alone maybe," he blurted out. *"Some even bring themselves to beg and in the last elections I sponsored hundreds of them,"* he revealed.

I honestly did not have words to tell such a disingenuous incompetent commander of the Land Forces whose only qualification is being sired by the president, whom he owes all the raw ranks and glory. He boasts around with empty intellectualism which isn't acquired from philosophy books or school, but from reading sycophants praising his father and other bloodsucking criminals. I emphasized to him that I do not criticize the government because I want such material benefits, but because of my decent respect for rule of law and good governance. One cannot genuinely fight against injustice and then begin to praise it because he has received material benefits. I would never compromise my conscience by bum-licking the demons that have made life difficult for everyone except themselves.

I told him that I am only attached to responsibility and not material possessions. He did not answer nor ask more questions about it. Instead, he asked me the size of my clothes.

"These ones I am wearing are not my clothes and I do not know their size," I said.

"I am buying you new clothes. We are releasing you," he said.

He looked at me with hate and arrogance flashing from his eyes. At that moment, I could see his mouth just moving in the middle of an overgrown beard and mustache, opening and closing like an arsehole after farting.

The hate I had for this man was justifiable, if only he knew what I was thinking about him. I was just there interacting with a pure devil. I was unfortunate to meet Satan but at least I lived to tell a story. Those who have been tortured by Museveni and his son Muhoozi know that they refused to be in political bed with him and he'll always use any means to suppress them. Leave alone the ambidextrous politicians who masquerade around as opposition for formality yet at night or secretly dine with the oppressors.

"I came with clothes, sir," I said.

"No, you are an important person so you must appear smart so I will buy you clothes which you will wear leaving this place, now that I have forgiven you," he said.

"What happened to the clothes I came with?" I asked.

"Stop asking stupid questions?" he said.

"Alright," I capitulated.

There was no need to trade in otiose and frivolous conversation with an intellectually bankrupt, coddled adult.

"Trouser 36 waist and 46 length. Shirt, I wear double extra-large," I answered.

He noted down on paper. He slurped up the contents of his cup in a swig and sighed.

"You will cooperate. We need to work together and develop our country," he said.

The way he was slurping up tea or porridge from his cup, I could see a pure simulacrum of his despot father in him. Pure evil, I thought, if only he knew what I thought of him. He is disastrously unanswerable.

In April 2020, when I was taken to Chieftaincy of Military Intelligence, I was taken to another posh house whose location I cannot tell, and met his father Yoweri Museveni. I was bold. I told him point

blank and our meeting came to an end unexpect-
edly.

"Whe-whe-where do you come from?" he asked staccato. He looked at me with inscrutable eyes.

"I come from Rukungiri," I answered.

"Whe-where... eh.. ekyizakyiti-ti-ti-re (exactly)?" He
asked again in a staccato-ed Runyankore accent.

*"In the neighborhood of your other pulchritudinous
diastema-ed lady-love paramour Kukunda,"* I answered.

He was now clearly discomfited by my stinging response and attempted to steal a glance at his wife
who was ensconced in a leather couch over yonder.
Her eyes were wide open transfixed at her consort
like a surprised clucky fowl.

There was silence for five minutes.

"Konka abantu ba' Rukungiri Mukabakyi mtche?"
(What is wrong with people from Rukungiri?)

*"Wewe kadogo, njoo umchukue huyu kijana (You
young man, come and take this boy),"* he said.

"I thought we were still talking, Mzee," I said.

Then I was grabbed by the ears and pulled like a
sack of rubbish out of the deluxe office.

Here I was now with his son Muhoozi, who appeared to be more brutal than his father and I couldn't dare speak my mind.

The following day, I was taken to him again in the same office. He wore a maroon polo shirt and sat in the same position which he was in the day before. After I had sat down, he threw the clothes at me and instructed me to put them on. A khaki trouser, gray hooded jumper, white vest, checkered boxers and a checkered shirt. They smelled new and looked expensive, except the underwear and vest which looked very cheap and not my standard. The crook must have bought the former in one of the expensive malls in Entebbe City and picked the latter from a rummage heap somewhere on the street.

"Do you fear to be seen naked?" he asked. His face and voice were not friendly. The way his eyes were not blinking and transfixed on my penis, I wondered if he wanted to see whether it was synonymous with my height. I suspected that he had already seen when they were torturing me days before.

If it were not for the swollen ankles, the clothes fitted me very well. I did not need to remove them. He handed me a paper to write my phone number and that of my wife. He promised to call me sometime to meet for a drink or dinner. I thanked him for the new clothes.

Did he get money from his pocket and buy these clothes, I wondered, or such expenses fall into the classified military budget? Imagine the huge budget that the finance ministry apportions to the military and it is rather spent on such operations of running torture chambers!

SPECIAL INVESTIGATIONS UNIT

My open shoes, spectacles, ring and wallet were brought. I was handcuffed and blindfolded again. The twilight was around the corner and I wondered where they were taking me at that time. Were they taking me back home? It was past court time. When I was led into a waiting car, I smiled. I trusted the hoodlum who had just bought me clothes and announced that he had forgiven me – I didn't know for what. As far as I was concerned, I had not committed any crime and hating someone has never been a crime either. It is a court which has the jurisdiction to rule whether someone's writing is in accordance with the laws but not the filthy barbarians in army uniform, armed with guns, who subject opinion makers or thinkers to mob justice. I did not know the day of the week or date, but I guessed that it was a Monday and we were at least ten days into the new year. I began calculating in my head from the day I was brought to the barracks, on 28th December 2021.

I was driven for almost two hours, the jam seemed to have been a lot. When the blindfold was removed and I was asked to get out of the car, I realized that I was at the Special Investigations Unit in Kireka. I had been to this place several times as a prisoner of conscience. When Afande Isingoma saw me, he smiled and shook his head.

"My friend, you are always in trouble on Whatsapp," he said. I had been in the white drone together with two other boys with whom they had brought us now to SIU.

The handcuffs were removed and we were ushered in a small room which is a waiting area for the cells.

"Cells are full, you will sleep here until tomorrow morning," said Isingoma.

"But Kakwenza you have dominated the news for two weeks now, why don't you leave these people alone? You are still young and should be patient as surely they will go," he added.

"Afande, leave me alone. I want to sleep on a thick mattress tonight," I said. Him and I had always joked. In my previous book (Banana Republic) I had written about him and he was happy that I had said everything as it was at SIU.

I was given a mattress and blanket, and my colleagues were also given one. I was to sleep alone on one mattress and they shared one. We were shown a jumbo bottle of water in the corner and a small green bucket in another corner where to urinate. He bade us goodnight and locked the heavy metal door.

I learned that my fellow victims of torture had been in the military detention center for almost a year! They had been dancing and beaten for all these months and they had given up on life. This was their first time to have a decent sleep from the time they were picked from their homes. One had been picked from Mityana district in central Uganda and another one from the eastern district of Busia, during elections. They told me their names and I vowed to at least make sure they get justice if I get released the following day. But events that unfolded later were not favorable and by the time I wrote this book, in exile, I had forgotten their names.

The wounds were still fresh to be encased in clothes. The heat from my body made them almost septic. I had been bundled into a car and sat on the wounds on my bums. By the time I got out, the trousers had stuck in. The night at SIU Kireka was a sad one as the clothes would again stick in the wounds which were now oozing pus and itching all the time. The ones on my thighs, which were as a result of plier plucking, would break and bleed upon any friction, since the thighs are very soft. Walking would be very difficult to avoid rubbing them together. I was better off naked.

On the early morning of 11th January, Isingoma woke us up. He said if we needed to bathe, there was a bathroom behind and that I specifically should do everything quickly because they were picking me up in a few. I was used to such – that is, the army dropping me from the torture chamber to here at SIU and then court or release on bond.

I did not know where they were taking me now. But since Muhoozi had said that they were releasing me, I thought that I would either be released on bond or taken to court and charged formally and then released on bail. Considering that I was in a very bad state, tortured, and held incommunicado beyond the constitutionally inviolable rule of 48-hours, I knew that at least the courts would have shame and protect my rights. Either way I was happy that I was no longer in military detention. That place is hell. I highly doubt that there is any hell or heaven after death. The real hell is right here on earth. Evil brutes like Museveni and his son are the devil and demons, while good and kind folks are the angels.

The military detention, where I was held and tortured, was illegal and offends the law. Article 23 (2) of the 1995 Constitution of Uganda provides that a person arrested, restricted or detained shall be kept in a place authorized by law. My captors acted like they were above the law.

Bill Ndyamuhaki showed up in a SUV Land Cruiser 79, grey double cabin pick up, and I was handcuffed and made to sit in the cabin between two masked and armed bodyguards in civilian clothes. Bill sat in the co-driver's seat and about six Police officers sat in the welded rear seats. I saw the other two boys being bundled into the drone which had brought us the previous night. I had no idea where they were being taken.

There was a police lead car with sirens being driven at bottleneck speed, clearing the way for the one I was in. Behind us was a white drone following with full lights on. Through the city jam, we arrived at Buganda Road Court at about 7:30 am and spent lots of time in the parking lot with the bodyguards who were reticent and busy on their smartphones. Bill Ndyamuhaki moved out with files and sauntered into the court building. I wondered what he was doing in the court building at 7 am yet court officially opens at 9 am. He was most likely cooking up something together with the nomenklatura rogues in the judiciary.

SMUGGLED INTO COURT

On 11th of January 2022, I was smuggled to Buganda Road court at 8:30 am or thereabout where the Chief Magistrate, Dr. Douglas Singiza presided over the most unfortunate illegalities that encapsulated the two bogus cases of disturbing the peace of Gen. Museveni and offensive communication against his son and commander of land forces, Gen. Muhoozi Kainerugaba, which were preferred against me.

I stood in the dock and watched the Magistrate and his two prosecutors, Joan Keko and Peter Mugisha, make fools of themselves as if they have never been to a law school and understood anything like human rights law or constitutional law. We were only four in the big courtroom, it wasn't the official time for the opening, I was simply smuggled in.

"My lord, none of my relatives nor my lawyer has been informed that I am here. My lawyer's office is just opposite this court," I pleaded.

"You are hereby remanded to Kitalya Mini Maximum Prison or Luzira Maximum Prison up to 21st of January 2022," he declared.

"My lord, I have been badly tortured as you can see, I need to be given bail and go to the hospital. I can undress and show you my whole body," I pleaded.

"We have a young woman over there and she wouldn't be pleased with your body. I will write to the prison authorities to supply me with your medical report in three days," he announced through his huge diastema, looking like a vacant plot of land in the Katanga slum as seen from above.

I was betrayed by the court which was supposed to observe my rights and freedom from inhuman treatment, torture and illegal detention. The magistrate provided a platform as a citadel for the rogue regime to showcase barbarism and all the oppression, which goes against the Uganda Code of Judicial Conduct. He ought to have known that his office was sacred as far as upholding the rule of law is concerned, but his grotesque judicial misconduct in sanitizing gross human rights abuses shocked me. I cried.

A magistrate with a doctorate in Public Law from the prestigious University of Western Cape, and a master's degree in Human Rights from the prestigious University of Pretoria, Douglas Singiza, whom I expected to be a justice aficionado, to my chagrin, his actions of whittling down my prayer proved otherwise. He was in bed with my tormentors as their chamcha. He ignored the law on torture and in lieu sent me to rot in prison.

From 28th December 2022, when I was subjected to unwarranted and violent arrest and torture, to the time I was produced in his court two weeks later, my tormentors had ignored the inviolable writ of habeas corpus commanding them to produce me to courts of law or release me unconditionally. I had been held incommunicado for more than the constitutionally mandated 48 hours rule.

I couldn't believe the bespectacled magistrate charging me pursuant to Section 25 of the computer misuse Act, legislated to protect government officials from criticism. His big head was not only bereft of the law, but also basic logic and humanity. The magistrate only needed to summon his senses and enforce the human rights laws as encapsulated in the statutes and stay the proceedings in lieu of sending me to Kitalya Mini Maximum prison. I prayed to him to permit me to undress and he saw the wounds crisscrossing my back, thighs, arms, buttocks, legs, and he erroneously whittled down my plea.

That was a miscarriage of justice. I cannot say that he erred in law. He proved to be in the same caboodle of my tormentors to proliferate political persecution yet his role as a judicial officer is to dispense justice with utmost impartiality. He ought to have accessed his full thinking capacity to dispense justice as he is obliged to. He would have discontinued the balderdash of the criminal proceedings against me but alas, these are our 21st century elites who boast around with degrees, but their professionalism depict otherwise.

He went to school and studied law, went on to the Law Development Center (LDC) and graduated as an advocate of the high court and subordinate courts thereto, recruited to judiciary as a chamcha of the rogue regime. I was told that before he joined the judiciary, he was teaching law! I am discombobulated about what kind of law he was teaching his students when he is such a chamcha of the higher authority who were interested in encasing me into oppression and persecution, yet the laws are supposed to protect me.

The constitutionally irrefragable responsibility of the Ugandan judiciary to protect citizens against the unlawful or arbitrary acts of the Army and Police has dwindled and the honorable Chief Justice, Owiny Dollo Alphonse, owes us a good explanation as to why he must not voluntarily bow out from his office rather than continuing to head an institution that is docile. The Ugandan judiciary is an institution that has unfortunately become acquiescent to external arm-twisting in total disregard of its Constitutionally mandated independence.

The long rumored invisible hand of the deep state in external subjugation is now visible and has unscrupulously nibbled away at the independence of the third arm of the government. Lately the barbarism of the state flourishes without being checked by the judiciary.

It is undoubtedly proven that only an independent judiciary can protect citizens from arbitrary state impunity and that doesn't require rocket science for any judicial officer to fathom. Conceivably, the problem is that these judicial officers may want to act in such a manner in order to be coddled by the *'deity'* that benefits from such an ensnared judiciary.

We, the citizens of Uganda, have nowhere to run to anymore when we are continuously enfolded in the state's labyrinth of failure to honor its obligations as elucidated in the social contract.

The constitution of the Republic of Uganda 1995 as amended recognizes the tripartite structure and independence of state institutions – the executive, judiciary and legislature – but the judiciary has become another appurtenance of the executive.

Lately, there is this barbaric method that the state is using against the disgruntled citizens who blow off steam protesting the negligence and oppression. When we are violently kidnapped and bundled into waiting numberless drones, we are not taken to Cafe Javas to eat Pizza! We are driven into torture chambers where we are mutilated incommunicado in total disregard of the law. That is why they return us when we are half dead.

When we are then smuggled into these Courts after the inviolable 48-hour rule has elapsed, the magistrates fold hands and zip their mouths yet they are supposed to enforce the human rights laws.

Judicial officers like Douglas Singiza have turned courts into adjuncts of the deep state to proliferate abuses against victims of such insufferable barbarism by denying them bail, or if they pretend to care, they give victims absolutely unaffordable bail in order to deter or demoralize other citizens from holding the government accountable.

One of the respected law scientists of the 21st century and former justice of the Constitutional Court of the Federal Republic of Germany, Prof. Dr Michael Eichberger, once noted that the independent courts can only exist in a state governed by the rule of law, and the rule of law is not possible without an independent judiciary.

When you listen to such legal aficionado individuals elucidating the role of the judiciary in enforcing human rights and rule of law, and then look at our judicial officers in Uganda, you wonder when we shall ever extricate our country from the manacles of despicable injustice.

I reminisce that through my years in Law School, I never used any Ugandan constitutional case law as reference, because judicial decisions from Uganda – especially since 2000 – are not decided with upright minds but corrupt and subservient psyches.

These individuals have the machismo to masquerade around as honorable judicial officers when their actions depict dishonorable toadying. I have always wondered what would happen if they put the country first before themselves and their survival instincts.

Judicial officers beating drums for the state's impunity to bloom have greatly pilloried the judiciary as an institution and pinned it to the citadel of bias for the entire world to witness learned people turn a respectable arm of government into something akin to a council of fools. I do not think that their children will forgive them. I have done my part to write widely about their misconduct and in reputable newspapers so in this modern technology we are blessed with, such publications will live forever and it will be just a matter of a click to read their filthy unethical behaviors.

My tormentors had entered court with guns and were waiting for me at the dock exit where I was handcuffed and taken back to the SUV. I was taken to Kitalya Maximum Prison like a VIP, for the first time I felt important when I saw a convoy of military vehicles escorting me to prison at a bottleneck speed with the lead car screaming sirens and clearing the road. I had only seen ministers being driven that way to their offices to malinger and do nothing, here I was in the same, being driven to prison.

The adversarial legal system informs Uganda's criminal jurisprudence. This is the system in common law countries – which Uganda received from the British in 1900's. Two advocates; the defense and the prosecution attorney, argue the case before an independent jury or judge who attempt to determine the truth and eventually give a verdict or judgement.

The basic features of this system are; a neutral/independent judge or jury, presentation of evidence by each attorney and then the highly structured procedure.

The principles of fair trial in the criminal procedure in Uganda got warped in the blizzard of cadre prosecution and judges who trade egregious distortions of what the law says and a corollary of which, many innocent people are serving sentences or remanded in prisons for crimes which they did not commit and the real criminals are walking free. Evidentially, when there is a gross dereliction of impartiality of the judges, prosecution becomes speculative and ineffective and eventually the rights of suspects are trumped upon and are treated like criminals.

KITALYA MAXIMUM PRISON

The car's digital clock was blinking at 11:30 am when the convoy arrived at Kitalya Mini Maximum Prison – a so-called modern prison located in Wakiso District, central Uganda. The prison is built on hundreds of acres of government land. The Chinese were contracted to erect the facility with the aim of decongesting the main prison in Luzira. It accommodates over a thousand inmates – remandees and convicts. I have been to several prisons in Uganda but Kitalya is better than others.

When the convoy transporting me had arrived at the gate, the gateman instructed the lead car with armed and uniformed military and policemen to make a U-turn, and he allowed only the SUV in which I was being chauffeured to pass through the first tall gate. It roared slowly on the murram driveway which led into the razor wired and high walled mesh lot where it stopped and we alighted. Everything – the pavers, metallic doors, padlocks, walls, among others – looked new and clean. Prison wardens took their positions in the watchtowers on top of the buildings and looked to be attentive and alert full time. It looked like a maximum prison indeed. From the first gate to the cells, there are about fifteen gates. It is very difficult, even unimaginable and impossible to escape from Kitalya Prison.

By the time I was taken to the reception block for admission, I overheard a Capital FM anchor reading news about my remand. I wondered how they knew about it since there was no one in court except the judge and two prosecutors.

The prisoners were outside their cells loitering, some playing football and others basketball, while others sat in groups sunbathing or chatting away their prison misery.

Bill Ndyamuhaki bade goodbye to me with a UGX 20,000 crispy note of legal tender and also handed over everything of mine, like my wallet to the prison officers.

"You guys tortured me to almost death and now have dumped me here in this prison to rot? I shall rejoice when you die," I said to him.

"You will be fine," he said.

A prison warden who heard me curse questioned why I would rejoice upon the death of a fellow human being and wondered.

"Why would you wish other people death?" he asked.

"It is a sweet feeling when you outlive your tormentor. But since you have never been tormented, you will not understand," I said.

The prison officers were shocked that the court could remand someone as tortured as me. They looked at me in disbelief, and the chief gave me a paper to narrate everything as it happened before being brought to prison. This was done in order to wash off the blame from themselves in case questions arose as to who had tortured me and when. Photographs were taken, details fed into the prison admission book, and I was given a yellow shirt and shorts as uniform. A doctor from the main prison whom I later got to know as Dr. James Kisambu was called in to be on standby to examine me and he came the following day. He had to write a report to the court as it had been instructed by the crooked magistrate. He did write in his report everything as it was without mincing his words, because he was also shocked to see my youthful body crisscrossed with uncountable deep wounds. I remember his assistant, a clinician called Apollo Byamukama, attempted to count the scars and couldn't. The following day, he returned with several medicines for me to swallow, cream for the wounds and soap for the same. He was sympathetic and would check in oftentimes to talk to me.

I was given two caretakers to look after me the entire time I was there, onc would bring my food bought from the prison kitchen and hot water for pressing my wounds and swollen body. Then another would lay my bed, help me bathe and also wash for me. I will forever be grateful to these two gentlemen in whose care my wounds survived being septic.

I left Kitalya without eating their food because it looked weird and not appetizing at all. After harvesting the maize ear, they remove the husk and mill the cob with silk and kernel. That is why the posho is like a piece of half-baked brick. Surprisingly some prisoners love it. They say that it stays long in the stomach. And the longer the digestion process, the longer one takes to get hungry again– they reason.

At Kitalya, when you arrive sick, they isolate you to the sickbay and provide you with necessary care in their capacity, even though they lack medicine. When the body mass index (BMI) is below normal, they put you in isolation cells where you are fed on soya porridge and two eggs a day plus their usual posho and beans until you gain some weight. The normal ones go to what they call *'ekigaali'* and either way they also eat eggs, but they sleep many in the wards. The VIP's are also taken to isolation and given a separate cell, self-contained.

I had grown bushy shaggy hair and a beard. Immediately after the admission, they shaved my head and chin clean. I looked at myself in the mirror and looked like a teenager for the lack of any hair on my face.

When I would not be seated under the scorching sun peeling off the dried tissue off the wounds, I would go to the library and read a book or computer laboratory to play games. Almost everyone knew about me because my story had been broadcast every day on the television since the day I was arrested. Every ward in Kitalya has a television and prisoners watch news.

I met many friends; illiterate, literate, professionals, and among others. Mathew Kanyamunyu, whom I had read about in the newspapers and had never met in person, welcomed me and took very good care of me. He would make sure that I had everything and never lacked anything, including coffee and powdered milk. Oftentimes he would invite me in his room to talk about politics and literature while we ate bananas. He was studying accounting while in prison and had lots of books kept in boxes in his cell. I would borrow books from him to read. I would read a book almost every two days and be done. The Idea of Justice, Introduction to Philosophy, King Leopold's Ghost and several others are some that I read while in prison.

On a daily basis, I would receive visitors. The visitation days were limited to two days a week – that is Monday and Thursday – but my visitors would be allowed to come and see me every day from Monday to Friday. I remember the first visitor I received was my friend Jane Abola who, upon seeing the state I was in and wearing a funny prison yellow uniform, wailed. I had not shopped for anything and she came carrying for me groceries and other necessities, including cash. My lawyer, Eron Kiiza, came immediately too because we had not met since I was arrested. He was out there fighting my battles with the law and advocacy. I had never seen him speechless and withdrawn like the first day when he saw me in Kitalya. In fact, I could read his face from the exasperation that he was restraining himself from crying after seeing his client in such a state. He would later return to Kampala and appear on different radio and television channels to tell the world how badly I was tortured, and that if anyone saw how I was tortured, no one would criticize the government again.

The leader of opposition in parliament, Rt. Hon. Mathias Mpuga and a few members of parliament, Uganda Human Rights Commission led by the Late Fr. Simon Lokodo and Crispin Kaheru and others also checked on me. PEN-Zentrum Deutschland representative Konrad Hirsch, who brought for me an honorary membership was refused entry into prison because he had no printed negative covid test as it was the requirement. As a European, he had carried the digital copy on his phone and was

rejected by prison officers who were not used to such advanced methods of keeping documents. Many other people who would not like to be mentioned for security reasons, thronged the prison to check on me.

If I had not received the little care at Kitalya Prison, maybe I would have died. By the time I moved out of that prison, I had greatly improved, though the ankles were still swollen and I was still limping. The wounds had peeled off the coating and were just red fresh scars which were not painful. The most severe effect I was battling now was lack of body balance and also post-traumatic stress disorder. It was difficult for me to stand for more than two minutes without collapsing. I was very weak.

If you want to know about how the justice system is functioning in Uganda, you must go to the prisons and listen to the stories of helpless prisoners. The criminals are on the streets wandering about and doing more criminality while the innocent are kept away wrongly in prison. I am not saying that all the people in prison are innocent and did not commit the crime, but if there was a competent justice system free of procedural injustice, prisons would be decongested. There are several people who spend years on remand without being produced in the competent court for case hearing, contrary to the law. Others have no legal representation, do not know their rights and are just there wasting their lives and future.

In prison you will hear stories from suspects who were taken to court just because they could not afford paying some money to be released on police bond. Later, for lack of evidence or failure to investigate cases, the prosecutors visit prisons and ask them to do a pre-bargain in exchange for lesser sentences, only to be shocked with 30-years of imprisonment! Those who refuse to kowtow, remain on remand for years and are never produced in court for trial.

I found a colleague, Dr. Ashraf Agaba, a 28-year-old medical doctor with a degree in medicine and another in surgery, locked in prison over filthy charges of being in possession of military hardware. He intimated to me that he was only driving from work one evening and gave a lift to his relative who happens to be an army person, and upon alighting from the car, forgot his military jacket. When he was stopped by the traffic officers and they saw the jacket, they asked whether he was a military officer and he responded that it was for his relative who forgot it in the car. He was locked, military intelligence called and they picked him up for interrogation which lasted weeks. Then he was taken to the military court martial where he was denied bail and sent on remand. There he was, in prison when the country was short of medical doctors. The reason he was refused bail was that he portrayed himself as opposition on his social media accounts. He was never given a chance to call a lawyer or his brother the owner of the jacket.

Hundreds of other National Unity Platform (NUP) members were also arrested, tortured and charged in court martial in such a manner, that they were found wearing red berets of their party and that they look like the berets for the military.

If I did not have a lawyer who is a fighter, and many sympathizers and well wishers helping me, I would still be in prison now. At least I knew that I was the talk every day and PEN Centers across the world, media houses and other civil society organizations and foreign diplomatic missions like the European Union and USA government were concerned about my situation.

When the 10 days elapsed and I was supposed to be taken to court, I was instead produced through video teleconferencing from the prison live to the court where my lawyers produced evidence of torture, which included prison medical report and prayed that since my rights were trumped upon, the Magistrate would release me on bail and stay the proceedings and forward the file to the High Court in accordance with the law. But the magistrate would later extenuate that the submitted evidence was very big and that he needed time to study it, so he adjourned the bail application for more days. This fool of a Magistrate was not minding about my health as I needed extensive medical attention. He was like a robot being controlled from somewhere by my tormentors.

The day came and I was given a cash bail of UGX 500,000 cash and each of my sureties, UGX 10,000,000. My passport was deposited into court as a condition too. The sureties were: Anna Ashaba, counsel Bob Kaija, counsel Julius Galisonga and my former constitutional law lecturer, David Lewis Lubongoya. The conditions for granting bail were very tough. When I saw the magistrate demanding for my passport, I knew that my dreams to escape as I had planned while still in the military detention had flopped. It was a sad day for me. My wings had been clipped and such a condition came like chains to chain me in the country further.

I had to wait in prison until the court release order arrived so that I could get a gate pass to move out. I was happy that after a month in prison, I was able to get my temporary freedom and meet my family and friends. I sat in the sweltering hot sun and waited for my lawyers to bring the release order.

KIDNAPPED FROM PRISON

It was about 2:40 pm when I was escorted out of Kitalya Prison by one prison warden. We sauntered through the several tall, heavily guarded metal gates. The sun was sweltering hot outside, the wind was blowing insouciantly. I had spent almost two weeks at Kitalya Mini Maximum Prison. Two weeks before that, I had been in the Special Forces Command (SFC) detention, so the breeze of fresh air, the wind, the effect of undisrupted sunlight, the scent of flowering vegetation, were like subtle savour of a delicacy after long without.

As I limped out of the exit gate that encapsulates the prison buildings, towards the barrier gate, I wondered where my lawyer and relatives were waiting from since I had been told that they had brought the release order from court and had come to pick me. The warden in whose protection I was, confirmed to me that they were in the visitors' parking, 400 meters away from the gate, ensconced in the vehicles.

Something was not right.

When we were nearing the main barrier gate, to my chagrin and utter shock, I saw a double cabin pickup vehicle whose number plates were covered with newspapers, parked strategically at the gate and its engine humming. I instinctively knew that my tormentors had come back to re-arrest me now from the prison. Upon asking my escort to clarify about the suspicious vehicle idling where parking is prohibited, he feigned ignorance of it and instructed me to move across the barrier to where my relatives and lawyers had parked as he branched off to the unfinished doorless office block.

I was recalcitrant towards his order and instead limped back following him into the doorless office at the gate. Upon hirpling five strides, six men in civilian clothes emerged from the maize plantation over yonder and ran with indescribable rapidity and surrounded me. They were all masked and in filthy civilian clothes. They looked like mature street urchins and smelt stale urine. These people had spent days without bathing.

"What do you want from me?" I asked, angrily.

"Kakwenza, can you walk or?" their ring leader asked, without force or rudeness in his voice.

"Don't you see that I'm sick and limping?" I retorted.

The prison had colluded with the army to keep my friends and relatives and lawyer away such that they would kidnap me without anyone's attention.

The men lifted me up without further ado, albeit with care, and took me to the waiting double cabin pickup as though I was a tray of eggs or glass.

Two youths with smelly armpits and mouths armed with pistols sat on my either side. The malodorous stench of stale urine or sweat emanated from them and pervaded the enclosed car, filling my nostrils. It is as though they had spent weeks on such a barbaric mission of kidnaping people and had not visited a bathroom. More of these chamchas sat in the rear and the vehicle roared into life, dodging the main exit route of the prison near the parking where my people had been waiting.

In about 500 meters, we met two Military Police trucks full of uniformed red top officers and one of the trucks led the way with shrilling sirens. Our double cabin was in the middle and another truck followed behind us. They made me feel like the most feared person in Uganda. Every vehicle was fueled, each of the chamchas and military officers were given per diem – all taxpayers money wasted on one tall lanky 33-year-old broke bloke armed with a pen.

Through the dusty bumpy road that wound through remote verdant villages, we connected to the Wakiso district side and onto the tarmac where now I was driven at bottleneck speed up to Makindye Military Barracks in the outskirts of Kampala. This time they treated me differently. I wasn't beaten nor blindfolded. Through the whole journey, my bodyguards would even help me turn in the seat if I wanted to.

The sun was sinking beyond the Kampala fogged sky when the Double Cabin pickup pulled into the bushy lawn of Makindye Military barracks. Two lanky and smartly dressed officers in Military Police uniform helped me to alight from the car and ushered me into a two bedroomed house across. It was fully contained with old toilet and bathroom wares. One officer who wore a name tag that read Haggai handed me to a tall plump, dark-skinned lady with humongous bouncing succulent breasts. She handed me two pairs of red Military Police prison Uniforms, a bottle of water and instructed me to shower, put on a uniform and keep my clothes in the closet and then sleep.

"I am hungry. I need to eat, be told why I am here, I need to see a doctor and also communicate with my lawyer immediately," I said.

She sweetly looked at me with a Cheshire cat-like smile for a second and pulled out a small cheap button phone from her hip pocket and rang someone.

"He looks tough and unwell; we should call the doctor to examine him immediately," the plump lady said. Her voice was infused with staccato.

The officer who had been called immediately showed up in the bedroom in about five minutes, panting.

He looked more senior to the lady. I was seated on bed with wounded thighs out, scarred arm and swollen legs all visible. He reached closer and took a look. He appeared shocked, and upon looking at my back, he took a step back. He immediately swiped on his phone and rang the doctor who confirmed that he had moved out of the barracks. He was instructed to return quickly. There was an inviolable order in his voice.

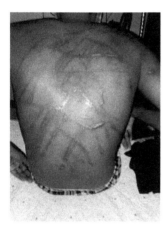 

When I was given a paper and pen to write down everything I needed in the house and the meals I would want to eat every day, I knew that the rogues had arrested me to keep me in Makindye Barracks for another month or more. Maybe they wanted my wounds to heal so that I appear less scarred in public.

I got the pen and paper and wrote down the food I would eat every day, and the drinks I needed at that moment. Then added a radio, shower gel, lotion and a shaver. All the requisition I made was brought in about thirty minutes. The food appeared to have been ordered from a hotel nearby. It was served on silver plates. Other items like coffee, soap, honey and others still had price tags. A box of water too was brought.

The doctor marched into the bedroom at about a half past seven, instructed me to undress and lay prostrate on the bed, and did a manual examination of me for about forty minutes. I could see the exasperation on his face when he saw my naked, scarred body and asked what had happened.

"I was beaten by your friends," I said.

"This is gross," he was discombobulated.

He matched out and made a phone call while walking in the corridor. I could hear him.

"This man is not in a good health condition to be here, please release him." He repeated *"please release him"* several times and his hoarse voice disappeared as he walked away.

At about 11 pm, Gen. Muhoozi Kinerugaba matched in wearing a maroon t-shirt tucked into gray khaki trousers. The black cape hid guilt in his eyes. The mustache was well combed and he looked relaxed as though he had been drinking the previous night. He stood with knock knees over yonder, holding his hands behind. Pure evil was following me again. I wondered what he wanted this time around. His distended belly looked compressed with a bulletproof trainer this time; it was not freely bouncing about like when I saw him a few days before.

"Kakwenza, I am here to finalize the deal with you," he said while sitting his whole obese self into a plastic chair by the bed.

"Which deal?" I feigned ignorance.

"Of the offers and not writing again," he retorted.

"I am not in the right mental and health state to respond now, but allow me to see my doctor and get medication then we'll talk," I begged.

"I do not want you to write about all this you went through and I am serious," he retorted.

I had sat on bed with the back leaned against the wall and legs hanging. I now sat on the edge with the legs down on the cemented ground.

"Okay," I lied.

"But no media, ok? Let me know in case you need anything," he said with a lot of dissatisfaction registered on his face.

"Now I am giving you an escort to your home, ok?" he said and marched out of the room.

"I am going to the hospital, not home." I protested.

He stood up and matched his elephantine bums out and without saying anything.

A few minutes later, the doctor returned and asked me to put on my clothes quickly. He stood in the middle of the bedroom as if to communicate the urgency of his communication. I gathered myself up and dressed up quickly as he instructed and I ambled behind him.

There was a white Toyota Corolla vehicle with number plates hidden with newspaper and I sat in it. The doctor sat on the left, a gunman sat on my right and another gunman sat in the co-driver's seat. The rickety car roared through the barracks and upon reaching the exit, a Military truck full of red tops led the way with sirens. There was another vehicle behind and a white drone. This was all taxpayers' money being wasted on me. The four vehicles that drove me all were fueled for a journey of more than 240 kilometers to Iganga and back. The soldiers were paid per diem.

For a moment I was scared. When the convoy didn't take me to the hospital and drove through the city and to Mukono, outside Kampala, I thought that they were taking me to be murdered and buried in Mabira or drowned in River Nile. Then we passed through the forest and via Jinja city.

At 3:30 am, I was dropped at my gate in Iganga and instructed to knock for my gateman to open. I tried to peep inside and the vehicle was not inside and wondered whether my wife had got scared and vacated the residence while I was in prison. My wife finally came, visibly terrified. They took pictures of me entering the gate and instructed me to close. They drove off.

I ensconced myself on the couch and she served me juice and bananas. The children were sleeping. The babysitter and the chambermaid came and welcomed me home.

"I am going to Kampala now. Where is the car?" I broke the silence.

"Please pack a t-shirt and trousers and give me some money if you have," I added.

"Sweetheart, in this state you are going to Kampala? You should sleep and I will take care of you," she countered.

"I know these crooks have not gone away and are lurking around to arrest me again. I must go to the hospital immediately because I am not well," I insisted.

My wife pitifully looked at me and couldn't understand what kind of human beings had inflicted such deep scars and suffering on me.

"I have been in court, and also came to the prison to pick you but we saw you being kidnapped again. Actually, I arrived here back from Kampala a few hours ago and the driver went with the vehicle," she explained.

"I have just seen a statement from the U.S. Embassy and also E.U. condemning your kidnap from prison," she said and handed me the phone to read.

She packed my bag and brought it to me, and she prayed for my safe journey.

In thirty minutes, the driver returned and was at the gate honking. I bade goodbye to my wife and off I went.

FOLLOWED EVERYWHERE

The first thing I did upon reaching Kampala City was to limp around searching for an open gadget shop to buy a phone. It was a cold morning and everyone was walking briskly to work and encased in sweaters and jackets. The sun was out already and still ineffectual. My phone had remained in the Military barracks and the one I had hidden was with a colleague somewhere in Kyanja for the landlord had evicted me out of the house when I was still in prison. I had no place to stay in the city and no mobile phone. When I went to the shop to buy a small button phone, I was told that it was a public holiday – Liberation Day. I couldn't get a sim card so I decided to get a special hire taxi to my friend's house so that I could get a phone.

26th January is the day the rogue regime celebrates liberation day. I always wonder what these hooligans liberated us from? They have done worse than the past regimes, but they masquerade around as liberators. In actual sense, they liberated themselves from poverty. They came preaching fundamental change and turned it into no change. They claim to have liberated the country 36 years ago yet die abroad seeking better medication 36 years later and return as cargo with international death certificates. They have betrayed the country and themselves. They are not heroes but villains. The greedy president, Yoweri Kaguta Museveni, upon capturing power said that the problem with Africa are leaders who overstay in power. By the time of writing this, he is making 40 years in power and doesn't want to go.

"Hello, can you please take me to Kyanja and then Kampala International Hospital?" I asked a random driver who had parked opposite Uganda House.

"Oh, yes. UGX 50,000," he agreed.

I sat in the co-driver's seat.

"Are you Kakwenza, the writer?" He recognized me.

"Sorry for everything. We have been following every day and praying for you," he added.

I avoided talking much with him because I was sleepy and lugubrious.

Upon dropping me to Kyanja, my friend advised him to go and that she would drive me to the hospital herself. Little did I know that I was being followed and immediately he drove into the road, he was apprehended and taken to Chieftaincy of Military Intelligence in Mbuya Barracks and interrogated about where he dropped me and how he knew me. He was released when they were satisfied that he was merely a driver picked randomly.

I came to know about all this when I reached the hospital and could not find my small phone. I returned to where I had picked him to ask if I had dropped it in his car. Upon seeing me, he almost chased me away and was very furious. He narrated to me how two military men riding on a bodaboda had intercepted him for hours and also took away my phone which had slipped out of my pocket into his car.

I kept changing hotels almost every two days, oftentimes getting an Airbnb until I fled the country.

After going to four different hospitals and all referring me to get medical attention abroad, I instructed my lawyer to apply to court so that I could get my confiscated passport and travel abroad for treatment. All the evidence in detail was submitted to court, but the foolish magistrate refused to release my passport and whittled down all the prayers reasoning that I would skip bail and run away from prosecution. It was no longer a prosecution but political persecution. He favored prosecution and persecution over my life.

In Nsambya hospital, The Surgery Naguru and others which I visited, I was diagnosed with a stress fracture of the left distal tibial shaft, periostitis left fibula, post-traumatic stress disorder (PTSD) and severe lacerations/dermatological ulcerations at various stages of healing. I had also lost about 15 kilograms and the doctor wondered what they did to me to lose such an enormous amount of weight in a month. By the time I was arrested, I was properly managing my weight between 90 to 95 kilograms. No more or less than that. I love to jog at least 10 km every day and I eat healthy organic or raw foodstuffs. I am a hypochondriac and loathe to grow a potbelly. The doctor was worried that I weighed 80 kilograms, and thus instructed me to begin eating meat until I return to 95 kilograms. It is true I was emaciated and my body mass index (BMI) was below the normal line. It took hours of convincing to accept his nutritional advice.

It was no longer a secret that I was no longer a wanted citizen. I was a pariah. Now the president and his son had used the judiciary to harass me. The institution which was supposed to protect me from state barbarism colluded with the state to encapsulate me into a destructible situation. I began to plan how to fly to Europe without a passport.

Upon reading a letter from the German Ambassador in Uganda addressed to him about the need to get my passport and travel to Germany for medication and receiving my honorary membership into PEN Deutschland, the Magistrate reasoned that the Ambassador breached diplomatic protocol by writing to the Court instead of the Ministry of Foreign affairs. A week later, Gen. Jeje Abubaker Odong, the Ugandan minister of foreign affairs, asked for a meeting with the Embassy officials to discuss the row and it ended prematurely with each stepping out.

MEETING ODREK RWABWOGO

Odrek Rwabwogo became Museveni's son in-law after marrying the latter's daughter, Patience Museveni. He is also the president's senior special advisor.

I had met with veteran journalist Timothy Kalyegira, who was brought to the law firm to take pictures and capture videos of my bruised body. Then Rwabwogo rang and asked to meet me urgently.

With an excess of Kinyankore accent in his voice, I couldn't doubt that he was the one since I had heard him several times in his fruitless hawking of National Resistance Movement (NRM) stale ideology.

"Yes, we can meet at our party offices in Najjanankumbi," I said.

"You well know that I cannot come to the Forum for Democratic Change (FDC) party office. We can meet somewhere in a hotel around the Central Business District," he protested.

"No please, we can meet at my lawyer's law firm at Master Plaza," I insisted.

He agreed to meet me the following day and I gave him proper directions with room number.

At 10 am, he showed up at the office together with his assistant, Mathew Bagonza, with whom we have been distant friends.

When you meet these two walking about together, you would think that it is Bagonza who is the boss of Rwabwogo. Odrek is bespectacled, lean with a flat tummy and always in out of fashion casual wear and passé winter boots, whereas his assistant is plump with a distended tummy and suave and clotheshorse.

He darted his inscrutable eyes about each corner of the office and finally grumbled that the office wasn't secure for a sensitive discussion.

"You could be having cameras and recording devices here," he said.

"Let us meet at Piato on Lumumba Avenue in about 15 minutes," he suggested.

My lawyer and I acquiesced to his dictatorship and arrogance, and we made it in time to the restaurant. After walking here and there looking for a safe place to meet, we finally found a quiet place in the verdant alfresco, under the shade of trees and sat there for an hour or two, talking.

At first he didn't believe my story and I threatened to walk away if he came all the way not to listen to me. The interjections were nauseating and with arrogance, a character of his clan. He must have got shocked because of the anger and *'I do not care attitude'* I showed him since such people in high echelons of power are used to being bumlicked and curtsed.

"But are you sure all this happens in this country and I do not know?" he asked foolishly with a mocking voice.

"You must be living on Mars," my lawyer interjected. I was about to ask who he is in this country to be knowing everything as it happens.

"But you Kakwenza you are too abusive in your communication; can't you tone down on that?" he asked.

"Does my unflattering language call for torture? And as a respectable lawyer, are you justifying such barbarism?" I asked.

"So, what are we going to do Kakwenza?" he asked. *"What is the way forward, because you have to forgive and we move on,"* he added.

I told him that we have totally different beliefs. Whereas he masquerades around as an ardent Christian and believes in forgiveness, I believe in revenge and I was not bound by his inherited dogmatic beliefs. I told him that hoodlums should not oppress others with hopes of running to colonial shrines to be forgiven when the offended are still grieving.

I told him that I am incorruptible and I would never kowtow to their incessant offers in exchange for my silence.

When we had finished, he asked that we go to the washrooms such that he sees the evidence of the torture. He took me to the toilets, locked the door and I undressed. He was shocked. He couldn't believe it. He promised that he would discuss it with the president and that he would get back to me.

I fled to exile without getting feedback from him, and he has never reached out to me again. I have always wondered how he approached his father in-law to talk about my torture, or if he had been sent by him to inveigle me into capitulation since Muhoozi Kainerugaba had failed flatly.

His sense of entitlement was stung when I told him that I believe in revenge and that I do not seek any material benefit from the junta. It seems he had never found a hot-headed person until he met me that day. If I were corruptible, I would never have reached such a level of being an unwanted citizen. I would be on a team of chamchas who traded their conscience for spewing balderdash in defense and sanitization of the junta.

A month later, I saw his boss and father in-law, despot Yoweri Museveni, addressing the inter-national press conference and blaming my torture on colonialism and that he was investigating it. What a foolish old man!

ESCAPING SURVILLENCE
AND FLEEING INTO EXILE

One of the high-ranking Special Forces Command (SFC) officer who participated in my grievous mutilation in the dreaded dungeons threatened that the only option I was left with was to kowtow to their demands and that I would live peacefully in Uganda like other critics who have been co-opted, swallowed and encapsulated in patronage. I itched to ask whether the capitulated comrades had been tortured like me before joining the dining table, but I feared to utter such thoughts. Conceivably my balls could have been skewered and roasted like chicken.

The brute who sounded like a Mukiga after breakfast on porridge and potatoes threatened that I would be exterminated like vermin together with my immediate family members. This kept haunting me to the marrow even when I came out of the dungeons.

"If you cannot accept and then go out there and begin from where you stopped in criticizing the government, we shall kill you, your immediate family members and that stupid lawyer of yours," he fumed.

"Even if you go out of the country, we shall find you and poison you," his voice kept ringing in my ears with fresh vibrance.

It is as though the dehumanization was a comeuppance of turning down their numerous offers since April 2020 when my horrendous woes with them began. Five times I have refused political appointments and gifts in order to cease fire and join the chamchas of the junta government.

My lawyer, Eron Kiiza, lumbered with another responsibility of being my bodyguard and big brother. From defending me in court, in media spaces and discussions, he really became part of my life and I owe him.

He would pick me up everyday in his ML Benz and take me to his law firm where I would spend the day, or chauffeur me to hospitals or to meet diplomats, and we would end the day at Serena or Sheraton to have dinner and a drink. Then he would drop me to my Airbnb at night. Whenever he was busy, he would delegate his friend and also a lawyer, Richard Baguma Rwatooro, with whom we studied law together at Cavendish Law School.

All this time, I would see filthy spies following us. Everywhere. Same faces at the hospitals, hotels, bars, parking lots, following on bodabodas. I would see them following us all the time, lurking around like shadows, but we pretended as though we were not seeing them.

Ignoring them also gave them confidence that I didn't know about the surveillance. They were not creative enough to predict my move, especially when the Magistrate refused to give me my passport, forward my file to the High Court, and said that once he begins hearing the case, it would be on a daily basis. He was after a quick conviction and I had to circumvent that. They were also stupid to think that without a passport and deploying empty-headed spies around me and red flagging me at all the border exit points, would deter me from fleeing the country.

On the day of escape, since they were used to my lawyer picking me in the morning and dropping me in the evening, I asked another person to pick me.

The apartment had many people with cars so the hired trolls were not smart enough to know which cars belonged in that gate and which new cars came in.

The goons were everywhere lurking around when I escaped unnoticed. They were at the junction as usual waiting to see my lawyer's Mercedes Benz drive by. I told my lawyer to drive there at the usual time just for formality, to hoodwink them and give them a wrong impression that I was still around so that we buy time for my fleeing.

Nine to ten hours later, my lawyer announced that I had fled and the sleepy *'intelligence'* officers wondered how I had made it out of their 24/7 surveillance and out of the country without a passport and through red flags at the airport and all exit points. My fleeing to exile caught them unawares and they believed it only after seeing my pictures while in Germany.

HOW I FLED TO GERMANY WITHOUT A PASSPORT

Sorry! Due to sensitivity of the information about how I made it out of Uganda without using the official borders and without my passport, and made it to Germany, this story will be available in a few years – as a separate book, but I can assure you that I have already written everything down and I will wait for the right time to publish it.

ARRIVAL IN GERMANY

I arrived in the Federal Republic of Germany during winter, nearing spring. It was a frost morning of 23rd February 2022 at Frankfurt International Airport, and the runways were glistening upon the Lufthansa Airbus touching down. Quite a humongous and busy airport it was at 5 am. I deplaned together with others, walked through the arrivals and lined up at the customs to be cleared by the immigration Police. The exercise was quick and efficient until I presented my passport for stamping.

"Who are you? Are you a president of an African country and have been overthrown and so you are here without your country's passport?" I was asked. He had to first call his bosses to inquire if I would be allowed in.

"He has the visa, why not? That is the most important," his superior acquiesced.

"In this passport and he doesn't speak Deutsch?" he asked, but the man had already walked away.

I marched out of the customs with a smile flickering across my face like a hologram. Even though I was relieved upon escaping out of the jaws of the crocodile mouth, my smile was like a sealed envelope harboring hate and rage against my tormen-tors.

Never have I hated anything in this world like Yoweri Kaguta Museveni and his son Muhoozi Kainerugaba. Whenever I look at my body and the badge of innumerable scars which will never disappear, I cry and pray that I outlive my tormentors and rejoice with pleasure upon their deaths. I do not think that there will be a room in my heart to forgive these outlaws and their batshit headed chamchas who behave like robots. I had escaped alone, leaving my little children and lovely wife still encapsulated in Uganda.

With a laptop bag slung on my shoulders, I climbed a flight of stairs following the signs to claim my baggage. The airport is very big and organized. I ran out of patience when I spent about 30 minutes with my eyes transfixed on the conveyor belt, and I could not see my bag while others scrambled for theirs. I had a few clothes and books therein, which I had bought somewhere in a third country. I got lost at first and wandered about looking for the arrivals gate where my contact had said he would stand waiting for me upon arrival.

After a few minutes of hopping in and out of many doors, I met Deniz Yücel, the then PEN-Zentrum Deutschland president, waiting for me. He stood near a pillar, head covered in a green beanie, himself encased in a black trench coat, jeans and sneakers. He had a shopping bag in the right hand and a cigarette in his right hand and pulled the last puff. When he saw me, he nipped and killed the burning cigarette and dropped the butt in the bin. Eyes brimmed with mirth and the smile tugging his lips broke into a grin. His smile was fatherly and genuine. When he gathered me into a hug, I felt the same warmth I used to get from my father before he paddled far beyond.

We burst out into boisterous, unrestrained and hearty laughter symbolic of the herculean journey I had endured to arrive in Germany.

"Great to meet you finally," I said happily.

"Great to see you, Kakwenza," he answered.

"Where is your luggage?" he asked.

"Ahh, I think we should just abandon it and go, I will buy new clothes," I said.

"No, let us go and look for it," he insisted.

It turned out that I was looking for my luggage on the wrong conveyor belt. He knew my arrival details and so he took me to the right belt where we found my decrepit bag. Others had picked their luggage and mine was there alone.

He had shopped for me clothes, including a winter jacket and he handed me the package immediately. The winter jacket was timely because the sky was overcast with clouds and frigid wind was blowing and the temperature was still down at negative one degree Celsius.

We smoked a cigarette, took a picture and broke the news that I had arrived safely in Germany. Throughout the whole journey to Bayern München, I was speaking on the phone giving interviews to journalists everywhere in the world.

I have met people everywhere in the world, but I had never met decent human beings whose actions depict magnanimity and benevolence like Deniz Yücel and Konrad Hirsch. These two gentlemen give a pure description of friendship, generosity and consideration. This is not to heap encomiums onto them for I know they are not saints, but as far as I understand the meaning of the African philosophy of Ubuntu, the duo deserve praise. Home is where you feel comfortable, they say, and I undoubtedly felt at home. I knew that I was safe and I was no longer going to be walking about watching over my shoulders to see whether I was being followed. The only worry I had was that of my family still being in Uganda.

Deniz drove me through the countryside on the magnificent highways, from Frankfurt to München where Konrad had prepared for me a whole fully furnished mansion by the lake in Seeshaupt to live until I settled in Germany. He knew that I loved to eat matooke, posho and beans and beer, so we found him and Edward Mutebi, his friend, in the kitchen downstairs cooking. They stayed around with me for two days, and when they were sure that I was capable of living alone, they left.

Prof. Carlos Collado-Seidel would often drive to the house and take me to Klinikum der Universität München for medical appointments with my doctor Vera Pederson – a lovely, experienced and friendly young doctor who wondered at the barbarism of African leaders who detest criticism! She pitifully, after looking at the wounds which decorated my body, asked how I could still afford to smile.

I had enough time to reflect on everything that happened to me since I was staying alone with no distractions. I would spend time reading all the news articles written about me while in prison. I had time to read a pile of books for intellectual nourishment. I would often times blow off my steam in the newspapers with stories of my torture. I learned how to cook and do chores for myself, among other things, courtesy of Hamidu Kakooza who was my frequent visitor and tour guide around the city of München when he wasn't in class studying for his master's degree. He's such an exquisite gentleman whose habitual liking for dancing and music infected and entertained me. Exile would have been boring if I had not met Hamidu.

Konrad didn't only do that, but also would introduce me to other wonderful friends like Lawyer Ronja Corell, with whom I would travel to Ausländerbehörde to apply for a Resident Permit.

I also met Edward Mutebi, an outstanding human rights activist who was studying his master's degree in Berlin. He's an excellent cook too whose food is compulsive. These friends together with my fellow exiled writer, Dr. Stella Nyanzi, who offered me motherly love and guidance in absence of my mother, were instrumental in my recuperation.

They gave me parental care and invaluable love which I needed to get back on my feet.

They became part of me and we became family. We eat, drink, fly and drive together for holidays to the sweltering hot European beaches dotted with conglomerate masses of nude flesh and pajamaed bodies baked to pink. We criticize each other and knock heads, among other things.

Konrad Hirsch took me to Schloss Bellevue, Federal Republic of Germany State House to meet the President, H.E. Frank-Walter Steinmeier and his wife, the First Lady, Elke Büdenbender. I handed him my book – Banana Republic: Where writing is treasonous – and he was overjoyed that I could give him a book to read.

WRITERS IN EXILE PROGRAM (WiE)

I will forever be grateful to this wonderful program of PEN-Zentrum Deutschland for having worked swiftly to welcome me as a scholar. This great program has been very important to me as a persecuted writer from Uganda. Together with other PEN centers worldwide, my rights and freedom were advocated for while I was in prison. When I was released and became a persona non grata in Uganda, at least I felt appreciated and loved somewhere away from my home country, from paying my bills to welcoming my wife and children to join me in Germany. This serves as an example that even if you do not agree with someone's opinion, at least defend their freedom to say or write it. Under the stewardship of an ex-prisoner of conscience, president Deniz Yücel, PEN-Zentrum Deutschland understood the dire situation I was enfolded in, and the swift need to be made an honorary member and eventually brought me to the safe haven.

I have had an opportunity to meet a number of persecuted writers who are also scholars of this program, and I must applaud the distinguished members of this organization, the staff and the government of the Federal Republic of Deutschland for giving us a chance to write our way to freedom without fear of our dictatorial governments subjectting us to bogus litigation, harassment and surveillance. Ever since I arrived here, I have been blowing off my steam and I am unstoppable. Not even the dozens of arrest warrants that were issued out against me and keep being renewed, will scare me.

Far from the sickening oppression and fear presently clouding over my home country, I feel that I am unstoppable and I will continue to write. I feel energized and fueled to shine more light in the hellholes of Uganda's junta leadership.

I am enthralled to live in a glorious country where freedom of expression and speech, the freedom to write–forms the bedrock of an outstanding model democracy. I do not have to worry that someone is lurking around to hack me, or that the government will come and kidnap me and subject me to harrowing torture just because I have written truth to power. For all the books I have written, I have been arrested, tortured and subjected to remote controlled courts of law but not anymore!

MY CULTURAL SHOCK

As an African who has spent many years in my motherland Uganda, apart from a few months I have lived in America, Canada and Britain, not everything in Germany and the whole of Europe came like a bolt from the blue. I had been shocked before in other parts of the world where I previously lived or visited. If 2021 and the year before had not been annus horribilis for me, I would never have imagined myself living in exile where, apparently, my returning home is dependent on the death or overthrow of the president and his son or myself selling my soul to the devil and capitulating to their whims and returning home to begin working for them. Here I am now in Europe, together with my little children and wife, displaced and without a modicum of an idea about ever returning to Uganda. Instead, I am getting acclimated to the new European culture of stoicism, striving for perfectionism and precision in all aspects – which traits will also be imbued in my junior Kakwenza's.

One of the things I have learnt about culture is that it does not make people, people make it — as succinctly written by Chimamanda Ngozi Adichie in her book *We should All Be Feminists*. I have seen different valued cultural practices and what used to be cherished beliefs disappear at the realization that such were rebarbative and not corroborating with the contemporary and evolving world, especially at the reception of the English Common Law. At the same time, I have been a witness to cherished dogmatic beliefs being replaced by other caricatures of dogmas packaged as civilization whereas there is no difference between the repulsive culture and/or beliefs and the accepted one.

Before colonists came to Mpororo Kingdom, my forefathers worshiped Ruhanga (the creator) through mediums (spirits). Upon the coming of Caucasians, they declared our way of worshiping as barbaric and repugnant and so brought Christianity and told my ancestors that they were henceforth to worship God through the medium called Jesus Christ whom they allege that he was born of a virgin woman, lived for a few decades while practicing several miracles and later died and arose on the third day and that he went to heaven to live with God where they are together watching over the world as we sin. You will realize that the repulsive religion which they successfully ostracized and branded barbaric, in actual sense is a caricature of the accepted one since all worship God as the creator through a medium. I grew up hating the impudence of such twaddling bossy dogmas, despite being born of an evangelist father who lived most years of his life spreading the doctrine of such colonial religion. Now I live my life as a proud iconoclast and pantheist.

The customs and social behaviors of German people are spellbinding. As a person who cherishes literature, art, philosophy, logic, reason, and, of course, a beer, I felt like this is my home apart from their food which discombobulated me and up to now I eat Ugandan food.

The only thing which shook me upon arriving in Germany was the culture of nakedness or nudity in the parks and on the beach, but it took me a short time to adapt and accept the change. As a writer who loves to describe nakedness, I wrote a lot of my personal notes about different types of skin tones and textures, feminine and masculine body shapes, sexual organs of men and women; youthful, middle age, moribund, hair types, breasts that are pawpaw shaped, pear shaped, full round, succulent and chirpy, sagging and lifeless and others — which I doubt will ever be published anywhere.

One summer evening as I was doing my postprandial exercise through Tiergarten park in Berlin, my curious gaze fell on completely naked people — hundreds of them baking themselves under the hot summer sun. I had to first take a seat on the park bench and think about inquiring what the event was about. But I stacked the curiosity back in the scabbard as I never wanted to embarrass myself appearing as an ignorant newcomer or stranger. I would later ask my friends, Konrad and Edward, who intimated to me that it is a culture in the Eastern part of Germany to be naked often. In saunas, everyone is naked too unlike in Uganda where men cover their lower body with a shoal and women cover their buxomness and breasts, it is normal to be naked for some people.

Whereas it is abominable in Uganda for a son or daughter to see his or her father or mother naked, I saw on several beaches old men completely naked with their wives and children. When I married my wife, because we come from different cultures, I was shocked that in their tribe I cannot even shake the hands of my mother in-law or give her a hug as it is in mine. It is completely abominable to even come near her, for flimsy and repugnant cultural reasons, yet in my tribe we freely open arms and gather our in-laws into hugs. My tribe, Bahororo, is one of the fifty-four tribes of Uganda.

MANAGING SEVERE PTSD

Sometime in December 2020, I was driving on John Babiha (Acacia) Avenue from Kololo side, and while snailing across the mouth of Windsor Loop, there popped a Drone (Toyota Hiace van), full lights beaming into my car, driving out of the junction and keyed up to join my lane. It had been speeding on that uphill and suddenly came to a tire screeching halt because the restive chauffeur found jam in which I and several others were enmeshed. The people who had manned the dreaded van seemed to have been from kidnapping someone and rushing him or her to the dungeons for torture. That is how they drive, like madmen.

With that speed and full lights, the driver seemed to have exaggerated confidence of the untouchable chamcha on mission. All the windows were tinted except the windshield. Like a scalded cat, I forthwith recognized that a similar car had picked me from my home not once, and on that remembrance my heart shook like a leaf and almost skipped out the chest. The gear shifter wasn't in parking, and I had only halted the car with my foot on the brake pedal. I do not remember the indescribable speed with which I ran out of my own car like a bat out of hell. By the time I regained consciousness, the car had self-moved and knocked the one which I was following. The motorists swiftly came to my rescue from the other side of the road where I had taken cover. Those who saw the frightening drone and later recognized me were there to console me at that particular moment. That was the turning point. I realized that I was seated on a time bomb which was about to explode with me. I had been triggered many times, but I hadn't taken it seriously until that time.

Another day I was standing on the rooftop of Cavendish Law School talking on the phone. Then a military vehicle drove through Bukoto street, speeding with shrieking sirens and all the beastly understanding of the narrowness of the road. I almost fell from the rooftop of the building out of fear. I thought that the army had located me and had come to bundle and drive me away for another scalding tirade of torture.

Later that evening, while walking to where I had parked my car on the same street, two armed men in Uganda People's Defense Forces (UPDF) uniform were casually maundering by, and upon seeing them, I almost rammed into an electric pole while attempting to run away from them yet they were going about their business. The fear of military vehicles, personnel and anything related to my tormentors was by reflex. My body would just react without consulting my brain.

Just like that, I would have fallen from the rooftop or rammed into an over speeding car and died without knowing that I was suffering from severe PTSD.

Oftentimes I would become a somnambulist. In the middle of the night I begin sleep-fighting and walking around the house — fighting gunmen encased in Special Forces Command (SFC) uniform. I was nearing that stage of walking out of the house and running on the streets in Adam's suit. I remember planning a weekend to Entebbe City to rest. Upon arrival, I was welcomed by billboards of Gen. Yoweri Museveni everywhere. The feeling of seeing a brutal despot on whose orders I have suffered greatly, stimulated deep distressing memories and so I made a U-turn and drove back to Kampala.

That despicable situation was being handled. By the time I was re-arrested in December 2021, I had been meeting a psychologist, Dr. Simon Ndawula, who used his expertise to make sure that I become a normal human being again, bereft of mental and emotional stress inflicted on me by my tormentors.

The situation worsened, again, when I fled into exile. This time it was not triggered by the presence of the military on the streets or convoys, because in Europe you hardly see any, but by my scarred body and incessant nightmares.

One time I covered all the mirrors in the house in order to avoid seeing myself, especially in the bathroom and laundry room. I became addicted to sex, alcohol and spacecakes to sedate me to sleep. I would also self-medicate the pain because I dislike pharmaceutical sedatives.

I got extricated from such a dangerous situation when I was introduced to an Italian aficionado psychologist, Dr. Mauro D'Ascanio, in Berlin, who professionally took me through a series of psychotherapy until everything began to move well with me, especially concentration and sleep disorder. I no longer get irritated or angered easily by people around me like before when I lost many friends that couldn't put up with my weird new behavior contrary to the natural charisma to which they had been used.

However much I am advised to forgive my tormentors and move on, it is very difficult to do as long as they are still alive and doing the same things or worse to many other people and thus creating thousands of other victims. The things that take place in the torture chambers, very few people have come out to speak or write about them. Horrendous things happen there and some are beyond any form of description. To imagine that they are done by human beings just to keep another human being in power is proof that the world is full of people but bereft of human beings. The people who man these torture chambers also have children, wives, siblings and relatives. Some victims come back and decide to keep quiet forever. But for me, I believe that blowing off the steam through writing about it is another form of therapy. Even when they die, that is if I outlive them, I will jubilate and rejoice, aware that justice was denied to me while they lived but their expiry has now released me from the bondage of helplessness.

WRITING TO THE JUDICIAL SERVICE COMMISSION

The injustice I was subjected to by the Chief Magistrate of Buganda Road Court is unspeakable in the legal circles. Any person who studied Law and has logic would never preside over such illegalities. It was a scandal. I had confidence that at least I would get a response from the body which takes in complaints, so I crafted a complaint and sent it through my lawyer.

Date: 23/5/2022

FROM: *Kakwenza Rukirabashaija*
               Kleine Alexanderstr. 8, Berlin
               Germany
               info@kakwenza.de

TO: *The Secretary,*
               Judicial Service Commission
               Plot 16 Mackinnon Rd, Kampala,
               Uganda

Dear Secretary,

RE - UNPROFESSIONAL CONDUCT
OF DR. DOUGLAS SINGIZA
IN KLA-00-CR-CO-0024-2022:
UGANDA V KAKWENZA RUKIRABASHAIJA

I am writing to make a formal complaint against the above-named judicial officer who is currently presiding over my political persecution disguised as a trial at Buganda Road Chief Magistrates Court.

On 28th December 2021 at 3pm or thereabout, twenty armed men, some wearing UPDF uniform and others in civilian clothes, unwarrantedly broke into my house on Arches Close in Kisaasi, Kampala. They beat me up with gun butts and kicks and punches, confiscated my phone, blindfolded me and drove me to Special Forces Command (SFC) dungeons in Entebbe where I was illegally detained for 14 days and while there, I was subjected to grievous and dreadful torture.

My captors did not follow any law in the entire 14 days I was in their captivity. I did not talk to my lawyer nor did I speak to any of my people as provided for in the Constitution of the Republic of Uganda 1995 as amended and other statutes pari materia. They tortured me incommunicado.

On 4th January, 2022, a court, presided over by Her Worship Irene Nambatya of the Chief Magistrate's court at Makindye, ruled my incommunicado detention illegal and ordered that I should be unconditionally released. Her ruling was stamped with a respected judiciary seal and an edict to every security officer to comply in respect of the independence of the judiciary. The order was looked at with repulsive and disgusting eyes, a desecration of the power of the judiciary in enforcement of human rights.

It is so sickening a fact that the judiciary did not do anything about such acts that undermine its constitutionally recognized independence. Instead, my captors reacted to such an inviolable order by driving me to Eastern Uganda in my Iganga Municipality home, where they turned everything in the house upside down for hours, searching for guns unwarrantedly.

On 11th January, 2022, I was smuggled into Buganda Road Court at 8:30am where Dr. Singiza Douglas presided over the most unfortunate illegalities and hence gave a platform for the abuse of my human dignity and the judicial function. I was charged with disturbing the peace of the president and offensive communication against his son Muhoozi Kainerugaba who is also the commander of Land Forces of the UPDF.

Firstly, my lawyer Eron Kiiza of Kiiza & Mugisha Advocates, whose office is a stone throw away from the court premises, wasn't informed that I would be produced in court nor did court allow me to contact him. I raised the issue to the presiding Chief Magistrate, Dr. Singiza Douglas, but he whittled it down.

I was in court well before 9:00am with the Chief Magistrate and two prosecutors while my captors, ring-led by Bill Ndyamuhaki waited at the exit door with pistols tucked into their crotches. That was unfortunate.

Secondly, all my hands, ankles and joints were visibly swollen. My thighs, buttocks and back were oozing pus from the deep dermatological ulcerations inflicted on me during the 14 days I was in the SFC torture dungeons. I brought it to the Chief Magistrate's attention who witnessed my tortured condition but shockingly rushed to remand me to Kitalya Prison in total disregard of the domestic human rights laws and other regional, continental and international charters that Uganda is signatory to.

Lastly, after securing a costly bail of UGX.500,000, which came laced with tough conditions of depositing my passport to court and barring me from speaking about my torture, I was kidnapped by gunmen from Kitalya Prison and detained at Makindye Military Police Barracks and hours later I was dropped at my home in Iganga Municipality at 3:30am.

The Chief Magistrate ought to have presided over my case with utmost impartiality without appearing to have been remote-controlled by my tormentors like a robot hired to proliferate political persecution against me. His actions were against the Uganda Code of Judicial Conduct, which he MUST be subservient to as he dispenses justice.

Kitalya Mini Maximum Prison supplied court with all the evidence of torture.

The Uganda Human Rights Commission team led by the Fr. Simon Lokodo (RIP) and Crispin Kaheru visited me in prison and they confirmed torture. My lawyer visited me, confirmed torture and addressed court about it in a letter.

All the medical reports including scans confirm torture. I still bear torture marks and suffer mental trauma.

Here I am in exile lumbering with triple shackles of judicial harassment, political persecution and frail health from torture.

I understand that you are formally required to respond to my complaint and act accordingly against such a judicial officer whose actions do not dispense justice but cause great suffering to the victims of gross human rights violations. Actions of my tormentors offended the laws of this great country and Dr. Douglas Singiza gave them a judicial platform and beat drums for them to dance on the sacredness of the inviolable provisions of the law! He not only failed to report my torture as required by law but also condoned and worsened it by remanding me in a visibly tortured state contrary to logic and the law.

His failure to dispense justice with utmost impartiality as he is obliged to honor and sacrimentalize the tools entrusted with him by the judiciary, made me flee in fear from such enfolds of injustice. I am ready to bleed to death while fighting against such unscrupulous and ambidextrous individuals.

I am hoping for a swift response, hopefully in a week's time, on this case concerning a judicial officer who is supposed to be ethical and legal aficionado pursuant to his obligations as a judicial officer but practically behaves otherwise. I will not take his grotesque judicial misconduct with equanimity. I hope the Judicial Service Commission and the judiciary do not condone unprofessionalism of the Chief Magistrate to proliferate the injustices and suffering against me, Kakwenza Rukirabashaija.

The comeuppance, should you procrastinate this urgent matter or mishandle it, you will suffer local, regional, continental and international embarrassment through various media outlets.

If you need any more information regarding the above subject, feel free to reach me via my contacts.

This letter was received and stamped by all the responsible authorities: Uganda Law Society, The Law Council, Parliament, Ministry of Justice, Judicial Service Commission, Chief Justice, Uganda Human Rights commission, etcetera. But none has ever responded to it! Do they have any response? I doubt it. They must be guilty and ashamed.

The Constitutional Court of Uganda has on several occasions, especially in the case of Dr. Kiiza Besigye & Others VS The A G, Constitutional petition No. 07 of 2007, pronounced itself that a trial which is tainted by human rights violations and illegalities is a nullity and the accused persons under such a trial must be set free.

The honorable justices of that court ruled that:

"This Court cannot sanction any continued prosecution of the petitioners where during the proceedings, the human rights of the petitioners have been violated to the extent described above. No matter how strong the evidence against them may be, no fair trial can be achieved at any subsequent trial, which would be a waste of time and an abuse of Court process. There are dicta and holdings from cases in the Republic of Kenya which provide persuasive guidance to this Court. In case of Albanus Mwasia Mutua Vs. Republic of (Kenya) Criminal Appeal no. 120 of 2004 the Court of Appeal of Kenya held:

'At the end of the day it is the Courts to enforce the provisions of the Constitution otherwise there would be no reason for having those provisions in the first place. The jurisprudence which emerges from the case we have cited in the judgment appears to be that an unexplained violation of a Constitution right will normally result in an acquittal irrespective of the nature and strength of evidence which may be adduced in support of the change."

In Republic Vs. Amos Karuga Karatu (Kenya) High Court Cr. Case No. 12 of 2006 the Court per Makhandia, J categorically stated:

"The time is near for the Judiciary to rise to the occasion and reclaim its mantle by scrupulously applying the law that seeks to secure, enhance and protect the fundamental rights and freedoms of an accused person. A prosecution mounted in breach of the law is a violation of the rights of the accused and is therefore a nullity. It matters not the nature of the violation… it matters not the evidence available against him is overwhelming. As long as (there is violation of the rights of the accused person) the prosecution remains a nullity."

This call is very relevant to Courts in Uganda, because in the process of producing and presenting suspects in our Courts, the police and the prosecution do violate numerous constitutional rights of accused persons, yet even where such violations are brought to the notice of Courts, the prosecution go ahead as if nothing has gone amiss. We think it is high time the judiciary reclaimed its mantle and applied the law to protect fundamental rights and freedoms of our people as the constitution requires.

ARMTWISTED IMMIGRATION

Immigration had been arm-twisted to deny my children passports until I made a public outcry which they had to account for. After leaving the country, the anger was put on my four sureties who now faced criminal summons for failing to produce me in court in accordance with their assumed obligation which they owed the court when they stood surety for me to get bail. Skipping bail once, logically has never been a basis for issuing arrest warrants, but for Douglas Singiza, he could not wait for me to skip bail at least twice or thrice for him to issue arrest warrants. When he knew that I wouldn't return to his filthy court, his anger was now shifted to my sureties. We made sure that all the four paid the consideration to the court of UGX 40,000,000, so that they would be discharged of their obligations to me. Upon submitting the receipts in the court, my tormentors now shifted the anger to my children and wife by denying them passports.

The people manning the Passport Office in Kampala have an idiosyncratic belief that everyone is a chump. That is why when they messed with me and were caught right in the labyrinth, in flagrante delicto, thought it easy to call a press conference to attempt to sanitize themselves with more ruse. Here is what happened.

Sometime in March 2022, my wife and I provided the necessary documentation to the passport office in Kampala, including paying for the express fees, interviews and whatever, pursuant to the rules, such that our three children could acquire passports in a day or two as it is always.

I remember when I was renewing mine back in October 2020, I paid express fees and indeed in 24 hours I had been called to go and pick it. Well, that was last year. Several months later Buganda Road Court Magistrate, Douglas Singiza would arbitrarily confiscate it and refuse me from flying out for treatment of my broken limbs and mutilated body. I told him to eat it, and I fled to Germany on a 'witch's broom', like Harry Potter.

When I slipped from my tormentors unawares, now they thought they would put the anger against my family, holding my kids at ransom, such that they bait me back. Neither did such threats nor sending me several emissaries to placate me into their whims work. I continued blowing off my steam.

I personally contacted people I know inside the Passport Office in April who confirmed to me that my children's files were put aside on orders from the people they were not willing to expose to me. Obviously, my enemies are known by everyone and it did not surprise me that they had decided to involve my small children of 8, 4 and 2 years.

When I threatened to expose them in the media, they gave an extenuation that their machines were down and no passports were being printed at the moment and that I had to be patient. Of course, I couldn't be patient when I was out of the crocodile's mouth and my family was still stuck therein.

I even received innumerable pieces of advice to stop blowing off the steam on social media, so that the dust settles and then my kids get passports. I refused. I instead instructed my lawyer, Eron Kiiza, to handle the matter for their arbitrary actions offends laws like Article 29(2)(c) of the Constitution of the Republic of Uganda and Section 39 of the Uganda Citizenship and Immigration Control Act, Cap 66, which guarantees the right of every Ugandan Citizen to a passport. To that effect, my lawyer addressed the media, European Union, Uganda Human Rights Commission, and several other concerned parties.

Then the Internal Affairs Spokesperson, Simon Peter Mundeyi, when asked to explain, for public relation purposes, also called the press and lied to them that my children's passports had been delayed because their machine broke down. That was hogwash.

I know a few people who, during the period they say the passport machine had broken down, actually got their express passports in six hours. Well, I thought the colleagues were cooking me with lies until I had to sponsor my friend who actually made express payment at 8 am in the morning and by 3 pm in the afternoon of the same day had his passport. So it was utter bullshit that they were not processing passports.

Well, no one believed their public relation stunt cum ruse explaining why it took them four months to give my children passports. If I hadn't come out to blow off my steam with defiance, up to now they would be ensconced and farting in their palatable offices while taking bribes and orders from above to deny my minors travel documents in total disregard of the law.

My public outcry, just like I came out against torture, was the light that shone through their hellholes of impunity and exposed them as incompetent and subservient to orders like automatons. They had no reasonable defense until they were also told to use their technical issues to sanitize their suppression against my children.

The best thing immigration should have done was to apologize and return the express fee of three children since they failed to deliver in the required timing.

I would have forgiven them and moved on but their big heads and lies fathered my anger to write this and expose them.

MUHOOZI IS A FLOWERING SYMPTOM OF HIS FATHER'S STUPIDITY

Like a dingbat gronk wandering on the moors, so forlorn and useless, Gen. Muhoozi Kainerugaba's presidential aspirations are otiose and frivolous and should be taken with the contempt it deserves. No country in this 21st century deserves an uncivilized curmudgeon as a leader.

Presently, his influence as the commander of Land Forces, in an attempt to mansplain the army that is already patronized by his father, Gen. Yoweri Kaguta Museveni Tibuhaburwa has created divisions in the UPDF as many senior military officials consider him to be very stupid to hold such a position in the army. I shudder at the thought of such a crook to be Uganda's president.

While the dictator is so much aware that he is in that inevitable moribund stage of life, and the foolishness that has impoverished Uganda is withering, he saw it fit to tutor his son so that he could take over the ruins after his death.

As the father is in charge of co-opting dissidents and patronizing institutions to consolidate the grip on power and also stooging for the Western governments, the son is in charge of the torture chambers or dungeons where the critics who have refused to be co-opted or subjugated by the whims of placation are taken and tortured or killed in cold blood. Those who can escape end up in exile.

The duo has caused the insufferable terror after terror in their four decades of junta type of kleptocratic gerontocracy. Giving a chance to the baby dictator to assume presidency shall evolve into yet another unendurable rule. His aspiration for the highest office of the land is akin to an avalanche of rolling disaster.

Imagine a 48-year-old man who is allegedly an alumnus of the best schools in Sweden and Uganda, including military training at Sandhurst in England and Russia – a heap of lucrative academic and military credentials that do not corroborate with his intelligence and achievements. As Miguna Miguna once said, the only achievement of this empty-headed crook is having Gen. Yoweri Kaguta Museveni as his father. What utterance escapes out of his mouth is simply bereft of intellectualism and lacks any modicum of acuity that is expected of a leader.

It is barely incomprehensible that on his birthday, he drunk-read a speech of two minutes from his phone which was prepared for him by his chamchas who are always gaslighting him. He misconstrues such encomiums from the bankrolled fools and digests it to behave like a peacock high on Viagra.

Elsewhere in the world, where democracy is espoused, people rise to the political stratum of admiration after making important and moving speeches. But this coddled baby dictator, Muhoozi Kainerugaba, thinks that spewing balderdash for of glorifying violence will earn him adulation. Stupid daddy's boy.

For now, any appeal to Muhoozi's sense is useless because no man with a spark of honor and integrity would act like this genetically modified army officer whose qualification is only a declaration of idolatry of his moribund father. The worship of his crooked and indecorous father depicts utter impotence and fear.

It appears, by the look of things, that the Uganda People's Defense Forces are not happy with the rate at which the incompetent and spoon-fed son of the dictator gets ranks and promotions despite living a sedentary lifestyle of boozing.

Muhoozi will always carry the gene of barbarism from his father. As psychologists and psychiatrists would put it, a person's house is the root of their problems. Indeed, the former's problems are identified with his father, Gen. Yoweri Kaguta Museveni. It is a case of 'monkey see, monkeys do' kind of indoctrination.

It is said that when a son of the alligator emerges from the swamp to announce the inheritance to the alligator's throne, and the latter drums up support, *"don't doubt him."* The harbinger of doom does not carry a flag to announce his presence, we are indeed doomed. Gen. Muhoozi Kainerugaba is the vulture lurking to scavenge from the carcass of the father's ruins.

Gen. Museveni's cataclysmic rule since 1986 will forever be remembered in our history as a badge of national pain, misfortune and deliberate ruin. That is if we ever step out of these despicable ruins he has created to celebrate some other person's ascendency to the power.

The former Museveni won hearts of many and ascended to the presidency while preaching the end to corruption, extrajudicial murder, torture, nepotism, inequality, extravagant spending and other bad governance factors responsible for the abyss we are plunged in as a country. Little did many know that we were coddling a snake and now the real person whose character we barely knew has obviously done worse than the predecessors that he admonished as swine.

Arguably, we can now exonerate his predecessors and bring it to Museveni's attention that his cause was simply a deceptive song of the hungry with naked desires and sharp teeth to eat like a glutton, but disguised as a liberation struggle.

He has twice offended the constitutional obligation to relinquish power, and all the time subdued Ugandans with insufferable violence, terror and pogroms to instead consolidate power. We can all agree that if it wasn't violence and abrogation of the constitution, Museveni wouldn't be president now.

As Yoweri Museveni nears the inevitable moribund stage of life, we can clearly see the simulacrum of him in his curmudgeon son, Gen. Muhoozi Kainerugaba, who, by infection and lack of intellectual acuity and virtues of a leader, could protract and wire-draw the carnage and shambles.

A story is told of a ghost that was chasing a woman in the darkest forest and then the night lost the battle to the day spontaneously. The beams of the sun began to illuminate through the forest and the haunted woman breathed a sigh of relief. The ghost which was discombobulated at the spontaneous day break stood over yonder and said, "You have been able to escape from me tonight but there are more other nights and I will surely get you. Hehe..." You can imagine the facial expression of the hopeful ghost laughing hysterically.

The point is that we might escape from Yoweri Kaguta Museveni's presidency but fall into more other pandemonium since his son, Muhoozi Kainerugaba, who has been, for years, molded and groomed to carry on with the barbarism is warming up like the proverbial ghost waiting for another night to attack.

My philosophy of life comes from storytelling, and it is through such expression that I see the antidote of impunity. I have received enough punishment at the hands of Yoweri Museveni and his son Muhoozi because of using literature as means of social protest to expose impunity, but I will not stop until we enjoy the fruits of freedom in the pearl of Africa— Uganda.

The joy of freedom will continue to elude us if we fold our hands in despair, like spectators, while the ghost, Muhoozi Kainerugaba, lurks around like a vulture or voracious hyena to scavenge from the ruins of his father's presidency.

Every Ugandan including the rich like Patrick Bitature and Robert Kabushenga and the likes are presently scrimping to eke out a living and pay bills and debts. The appalling poverty is scattered everywhere and everyone is debt ridden including the government that we look up to to extricate us out of the impoverishment in which we are enmeshed.

Sadly, the impoverishment is caused by the same government we look up to.

Muhoozi Kainerugaba has been an enabler of the ruins of Gen. Museveni's presidency and a glorifier of the same. His apparent aspirations to take over from his father are not to do anything differently but rather to prolong his father's kleptocratic gerontocracy. Ugandans must be aware and say no to such kind of madness that is growing feathers.

USA CONSCIENCE-STRICKEN OVER FRATERNIZING WITH DESPOTS LIKE MUSEVENI

In December 2021, my article expressing utmost dissatisfaction of the ineffectual sanctions by the U.S. government against low-ranking military officers in Uganda in lieu of high-ranking ones due to incessant human rights abuses, was published by several newspapers.

Little did I know that it would attract the attention of those to whom it was targeted. Or, if it did, that I would receive feedback from respectable politicians from America.

A high-ranking U.S. politician — who seemed well conversant with the Greatlakes geopolitics — contacted me on Twitter to give feedback after reading the article.

To begin with, he was concerned and furious at the same time how the junta government of Uganda led by Gen. Yoweri Kaguta Museveni has been treating me since 2020. He confessed how he had spent his valuable time on my Wikipedia reading about me and gaping at the pictures of my mutilated body in the different newspapers.

After we had talked for hours, he asked me what the USA should do to help to correct the abhorrent cataclysm in Uganda. Often times, I have a template answer for such questions of how the Western governments can help Ugandans who have been subjected to insufferable terror by Gen. Yoweri Kaguta Museveni, who has been a U.S. puppet for close to 40-years now.

I told him that the US government is undoubtedly led by shameless hypocrites who loudly preach respect for the rule of law, democracy and human rights but silently support flagrant abusers of the same like Gen. Yoweri Museveni.

I brought it to his attention that there must be common values upon which the relationship between the US government and African leaders is bound, and offending such sacrosanct values should automatically discontinue the relationship and the entire support with which it comes.

The Military support Gen. Museveni enjoys is misused to terrorize the Ugandan people while the financial support is used to patronize and also squandered amongst themselves.

The U.S. Ambassy in Kampala only stops at issuing rhetoric statements as they continue to recognize the mad dictator. The high-ranking official reasoned that Gen. Yoweri Museveni is their stooge who is deemed critical in the war against militarized religious groups.

"Assuming Gen. Yoweri Kaguta Museveni was removed from power to allow for a transition to a

democratic republic of Uganda, how would the U.S. be assured that militarized religious groups would not seize power and or become a threat to the U.S.?" he asked.

I was incensed to hear that the high-ranking official, who preferred anonymity, would justify the U.S. government's overflowing support to dictator Yoweri Museveni on the basis of protecting American interests. It is as though he was conceding complicity of America in terrorizing Ugandans because of geopolitical expediency.

As long as dictator Museveni is being used by the U.S. government to fight their wars, they will keep supporting his harrowing barbarism in Uganda and we are on our own like ducklings. He can butcher us like pigs at the full watch of the West.

In other words, African acclaimed butchers like Gen. Museveni are good in the eyes of the Western governments as long as they are pawns lumbering with the responsibility of easing interests of their white masters at the sheer disregard of the laws and integrity.

The United States' hypocrisy takes me with chagrin, and I wonder why leaders of such a great nation preach water and then turn around to drink wine without shame. The claim of having noble beliefs than is the case actually stinks.

It doesn't make sense for the U.S government to vehemently condemn – and ask everyone in the world to do the same – Russia's arbitrary invasion of Ukraine and all the terror president Vladmir Putin has imposed onto the small country, and then on the other hand support the father of African murderous dictators called Gen. Yoweri Kaguta Museveni. This monster who is presiding over a mockery of democracy in Uganda is bankrolled by the U.S. and the latter watches on like a spectator as the former murders critics in cold blood. As long as he is stooging perfectly as expected, the values are put aside and he is never condemned.

Gen. Yoweri Kaguta Museveni is the monster that has been in power for almost 40 years and all this time his presidency has been characterized by kidnap, torture, displacement, enforced disappearance, mass murder, pogroms and other evils which are at the disposal of any experienced junta facing domestic resistance.

It is as though the continued USA support is to toast to this untold oppression, barbarism, sham elections – and to legitimize the rule of the greatest stooge as a token of encouragement and a job well done.

Dear USA, European Union and other democracies, have you no morals and shame to visit and rub shoulders with such demons? The governments which you represent and the UN have no shame not to act against these monsters who have no respect for values and international charters?

We as survivors of Gen. Museveni's terror are watching and taking notes as you preach human rights, rule of law, democracy, among other values, then turn around to eat your vomit, dine, toast and support abusers of the same values that you preach. What a shame!

We need answers beyond your foreign policy and interests. The answers that we need as victims must address why the US continues to support a flagrant abuser of rule of law, civil liberties and democracy which the American government espouses.

AFTERWORD
BY PROF. MILTON ALLIMADI

THIS MAN ACTUALLY BELIEVES
"THE PEN IS MIGHTIER THAN THE SWORD"

After being brutalized by the most evil terrorist regime Africa has ever known, General Yoweri Museveni's kleptocracy, Kakwenza Rukirabashaija is still on his feet and fighting to remove military tyranny from Uganda.

Writers determined to speak truth to power pay a very high price. Journalists and authors are unsafe in Africa. They are kidnapped, tortured, and killed. They are shot by the police and the armed forces. The police had standing orders to shoot to kill during Uganda's 2021 stolen elections. The body counts of Museveni's 37 years of tyranny amount to hundreds of thousands when we include those killed in periodic massacres and the war Museveni carried out for more than two decades in the northern part of Uganda. His victims are in the millions when we include the countries he's invaded.

But Museveni and his rotund and unintelligent son, General Muhoozi Kainerugaba, have never had to deal with a writer like Kakwenza. He grows another hand and keeps writing each time they chop it off.

There's really something wrong with this young Ugandan writer. He takes the saying *"the pen is mightier than the sword"* literally. Most people think it's just a cute sounding term.

When it comes to bravery, Kakwenza comes in the tradition of Kenya's Ngugi wa Thiong'o, one of the world's greatest writers.

Ngugi wanted to wake up Kenyans from their apathy. He was already a world-known established and successful author when in 1977 he co-wrote with Ngugi wa Mirii the play *"Ngaahika Ndeenda"* or *"I will marry when I want."* Ngugi wanted the masses to become actively involved, so his innovative theater promoted interaction with the performers.

Theater was no longer merely an intellectual bourgeois spectacle. The people now tasted the power of theater – they were becoming more conscious. They were learning the importance of questioning old traditions that prevented them from improving their lives. More importantly, they were learning the language and conduct that would equip them to demand more from their government: they were learning that their president was not an unassailable god or potentate. Governments are there to deliver services; not to plunder resources. Ngugi was arrested under the dictatorship of Daniel arap Moi and held without charges or trial for a year.

Global pressure led to his release and he fled to the United States. In 1981 Ngugi published "Detained" an account of his incarceration without trial.

Fast forward to our 21st century, in Kenya's neighbor, Uganda. Gen. Museveni's monstrous dictatorship is comparable to the barbaric racist dictatorships that once operated in apartheid South Africa and Rhodesia.

Those white minority regimes practiced race-discrimination. Museveni practices ethnic-apartheid; awarding top jobs in government, the diplomatic services and the military, as well as government scholarships and contracts mostly to *"his"* people. He really sees the rest of Uganda as made up of his *"enemies."* He has no political base and survives by his absolute control of the military, and, because he's a reliable puppet of the United States, he receives about $1 billion from Washington annually. Kwame Nkrumah had enemies of Africa like Museveni in mind when he wrote *"Neo-colonialism The Last Stage of Imperialism,"* in 1965. He warned of reactionary leaders who'd be sustained by foreign powers.

In addition to Ugandans, the victims of his militarism include the citizens of the countries he's invaded: Rwanda in 1990, the Congo multiple times beginning in 1996, and South Sudan in 2013.

Enter Kakwenza Rukirabashaija.

His first book, *"The Greedy Barbarian,"* was a fictionalized account of a corrupt African dictator who loots the national treasury. Museveni saw too much resemblance and had Rukirabashaija arrested and tortured by the military; the abuse included beatings, waterboarding, and being ordered to eat his feces which he rejected. Upon his release, Rukirabashaija authored *"Banana Republic – where writing is treasonous,"* he was again promptly arrested and tortured.

Rukirabashaija's fearless critique of the brutal regime was noticed by the outside world and he was awarded the PEN International Writer of Courage in 2020. But Museveni's backward regime knows no bounds. In late 2021 Rukirabashaija again earned the wrath of Museveni and Kainerugaba, or, as some Ugandans now refer to the pair *"Papa Doc and Baby Doc,"* – they are much more brutal than the late Duvaliers of Haiti. On that occasion Rukirabashaija had fired off some tweets referencing Gen. Kainerugaba's obesity. He'd frequently wondered how a general of the army could have such an ample belly, mid-section, breast, and rear-end.

The Museveni's went ballistic. This time the torture was so horrific – including lashes that left his back with ugly scars that resemble the kind of wounds on the backs of formerly-enslaved Africans in the United States – that before he was dragged to a sham court appearance, the regime's doctors had to give him medical treatment in the dungeons where he was being abused. There's no need for me to detail the abuse since that it the subject of the book you've just finished reading *"Savage Avengers."*

Many of his friends and fans inside and outside Uganda – including yours truly – denounced the regime's abuse of Rukirabashaija and lobbied Washington and the other capitals that continue to finance the regime of torture, bloodshed, and corruption in Uganda. PEN International also mobilized a global movement. Kakwenza lived to fight another day. If Africa's Papa Doc and Baby Doc had hoped to silence Kakwenza by ripping the flesh off his back, he has fired back with this account you've just read.

Kakwenza has taught Ugandans that there's nothing special about Museveni and Kainerugaba – if the junior dictator has fat buttocks because he won't go to the gym, Kakwenza believes Ugandans have the right to tweet about that – in addition to the corruption and tyranny.

General Museveni's regime continues to kidnap, torture, and rape Ugandans. But writers like Kakwenza, who now lives in exile in Europe, will not be silenced. He continues to expose the Museveni regime's monstrosity – this is the only hope for Uganda's liberation.

This is the only path to Uganda's liberation. The world would be far more unsafe for genocidal tyrants like Museveni if more of us follow Rukirabashaija's lead and start believing that, indeed, *"the pen is mightier than the sword."*

Prof. Milton Allimadi is a Ugandan-American author, journalist, professor and co-founder of "Black Star News." He ist known for his critique of racist writing by white authors about Africa and Africans. He is the author of "The Hearts of Darkness" about the history of Western media demonization of Africa.

When Bekunda and her toddler son, Kayibanda, cross an
international border, they are in dire straits and desper-
ately need sanctuary, human kindness and divine favor.
The new country gives them sanctuary, the natives show
them kindness and the local spirits do the miraculous on
their behalf. But can Kayibanda be as gracious to his new
country as it has been to him? Can he overcome his pro-
foundly awed nature, which appears to be hereditary?

Kakwenza Rukirabashaija
Thre Greedy Barbarian
192 pages, First Published in 2020
ISBN 978-3-9825132-0-1

www.kakwenza.de

2021 PEN International Writer of Courage Award

On 13th, April 2020, shortly after the publication of his first novel, *The Greedy Barbarian*, Kakwenza was arrested at his home in Iganga by security agents, detained and tortured for a week, at the military barracks in Mbuya. He was then arraigned in court on the charge of "*an act likely to spread the infection of disease (COVID-19), contrary to section 171 of the Penal Code Act, cap 120*", and remanded in custody to Busesa government prison. The charge was subsequently dismissed by the magistrate for lack of witnesses. In *Banana Republic*, Rukirabashaija describes his harrowing ordeal in the chambers of security agencies.

Kakwenza Rukirabashaija
Banana Republic – where writing is treasonous
125 pages, First Published in 2020
ISBN 978-3-9825132-4-9

www.kakwenza.de